PROPHETIC INSIGHT

The Higher Education and Pedagogy of African Americans

EARNEST N. BRACEY

University Press of America, Inc.
Lanham • New York • Oxford

Copyright © 1999 by
University Press of America,® Inc.
4720 Boston Way
Lanham, Maryland 20706

12 Hid's Copse Rd.
Cumnor Hill, Oxford OX2 9JJ

Library of Congress Cataloging-in-Publication Data

Bracey, Earnest N.
Prophetic insight : the higher education and pedagogy of African
Americans / Earnest N. Bracey.
p.   cm.
Includes bibliographical references and index.
1. Afro-Americans—Education (Higher)—Social aspects. 2. Afro-
American universities and colleges—Sociological aspects. 3.
Afrocentrism—United States. 4. Education, Higher—Aims and
objectives—United States.   I. Title.
LC2781.B73 1999 378'.0089'96073—dc21   99—22439 CIP

ISBN 0-7618-1383-7 (cloth: alk. ppr.)
ISBN 0-7618-1384-5- (pbk: alk. ppr.)

⊖™ The paper used in this publication meets the minimum
requirements of American National Standard for Information
Sciences—Permanence of Paper for Printed Library Materials,
ANSI Z39.48—1984

Dedicated To

My wife, Atsuko,
and my four sisters —

Maggie
Virginia (deceased)
Romella
Linda

Contents

Acknowledgments   vii

Chapter 1
Introduction   1
Chapter 2
Clash of the Black Titans:
W. E. B. DuBois and Booker T. Washington   9
Chapter 3
Crisis of the African American Student and the Development
of Historically Black Colleges and Universities   29
Chapter 4
Black Studies, and Black Feminism at Colleges
and Universities: The Curriculum Debate   47
Chapter 5
Molefi Kete Asante and the Legitimacy of Afrocentricity   63
Chapter 6
The Politics of Race in Higher Education
for African Americans   91
Chapter 7
The Future of Black Colleges and Universities
in the United States   109

Bibliography   127
Index   135
About the Author   145

Acknowledgments

I wish to express my profound gratitude to several *extraordinary* professors and scholars in the fields of psychology and education from *The Graduate School of America,* who provided constructive comments on earlier drafts of the various chapters in this book, in the form of separate essays: Manuel Woods, Sybil Anne McClary, and Robert C. Ford.

Since I came to Nevada five years ago, I have received advice and support from several people, as well as *unfailing* encouragement from several of my colleagues in the Department of Philosophical and Regional Studies at the *Community College of Southern Nevada* – in particular, Charles Okeke, Michael Green, Alan Balboni, John Hollitz, DeAnna Beachley, Larry Tomlinson, James Wallis, Guillermo Monkman, Gary E. Elliott, James Fuller and Taj Bakhshi – all of whom have inspired me with their camaraderie and friendship.

To say the least, the many months I have worked on this book has been a challenge, given that I taught a full load of undergraduate classes in political science. Therefore, without the interlibrary loan staff at the *Community College of Southern Nevada*, and, in particular, Marion Martin, this book would have been impossible. Out of sheer kindness, Marion Martin helped me find several of the rare sources listed in the bibliography of this work. Her patience and generosity always amazed me, and I am indebted to her, as her work was invaluable.

In addition, I want to thank Rita Roberts in the Department of Philosophical and Regional Studies for her assistance. Lastly, I want to thank my wife, Atsuko, for her support, as always, and my daughters, Princess, Dominique, and my son, Omar. I am grateful for their support.

Chapter One

ℰᴐᏃ

Introduction

The information and research imparted or presented in this book is both necessary and vital to our understanding of the past and present educational woes of African Americans in the United States today.

The first chapter about W. E. B. DuBois and Booker T. Washington in this work tries to point out the significance of studying histories of past educators to understand the future – or the influence and contribution important individuals have made to higher education – particularly in terms of educating African Americans in modern-day society. Indeed, what do historical time and circumstances have to do with understanding the present or future of our education in America? According to Richard E. Neustadt and Ernest R. May (1986, p. 246), "Perception of time-in-flow cannot help but be encouraged by purposeful study of stretches of history, regardless of whose it is or what the focus."

These considerations are important to understand because, as pointed out in chapter two of this text, "the turn of this century was marked by heated debate among conservative and radical blacks over the merits of vocational versus liberal arts education. The argument was epitomized in the divergent philosophical, political, and pedagogical views of the era's major black leaders, Booker T. Washington, and W. E. B. DuBois" (Roebuck and Komanduri S. Murty, 1993, p.30).

Toward this end, one must also note that higher education has not progressed to the extent of alleviating the segregation of Black and White students into two university systems throughout the United States, and fully including minority and ethnic studies in the college curriculum. However, arguing in his controversial bestseller, *The Closing of the American Mind*, the late Allan Bloom (1987, p. 245) stated that "there is one simple rule for the university's activity: it need not concern itself with providing its students with experiences that are available in democratic society. They will have them in any event. It must provide them with experiences they cannot have there."

As a black scholar and an African American, I totally disagree with Bloom's narrow thinking and the assertion that there is no place for the study of racial and ethnic groups on our universities, because the presence of minority and ethnic groups (or diverse curriculums), as well as other cultures, will only enrich all of our lives. As Paulo Freire (1972, pp. 68-69), the gifted Brazilian scholar, in his famous book *Pedagogy of the Oppressed*, has written:

> Students, as they are increasingly posed with problems relating to themselves in the world and with the world will feel increasingly challenged and obliged to respond to the challenge. Because they apprehend the challenge as interrelated to other problems within a total context, not as a theoretical question, the resulting comprehension tends to be increasingly critical and thus constantly less alienated. Their response to the challenge evokes new challenges; and gradually the students come to regard themselves as committed.

Some educators and critics would, nonetheless, argue that teaching multicultural subjects, as suggested in this book, and including racial and ethnic groups in Higher Education, as also advocated, "Challenge the balance among competing interests within the larger community and have the potential to fragment the political consensus upon which the American common school tradition rests: For when we cannot agree on what is legitimately a common curriculum, particular communities either seek refuge outside of the public system or seek to impose their values on the public system itself" (Applebee, 1996, p. 119).

Although we cannot allow for every subject or discipline (under the academic sun, so to speak) on American campuses, these things still should be provided for students as viable alternatives. If we don't provide these diverse things, are we saying students are not sophisticated enough to make the necessary decisions about these matters for themselves? According to Professor Terry Jones (1998, p. 28), "Diversity and affirmative action [in Higher Education] are not fuzzy, abstract, or altruistic goals: the well being of our society depends on them."

The chapter on Afrocentricity in this volume tells us that, for the most part, some white academicians continue to portray, as in the past, African Americans in an unflattering and stereotypical way. In other words, many historians' picture of black people's humanism is not always accurate or appealing.

Although Afrocentricity or Africology has been under intense scrutiny and criticism in recent years, the discipline allows black scholars, historians and journalists to write about *their* perspectives of those matters that concern African Americans and blacks who have been displaced from the continent of Africa around the world. In a complex and unique way, racial and ethnic studies, like Afrocentricity, seriously challenge the student's traditional understanding of national and international, as well as humanistic relationships, and not only in educational endeavors. It further gives the student an appreciation and knowledge of the complex and sophisticated world. As a consequence, such serious study of racial and ethnic groups, as demonstrated in this book, can also positively change the student's self-awareness, direction and perceptions about life. Professor Kieran Egan (1991, p. 3) writes:

> Education . . . is generally dreary because we have only three significant educational ideas: that we must shape the young to the current norms and conventions of adult society, that we must teach them the knowledge that will ensure their thinking conforms with what is real and true about the world, and that we must encourage the development of each student's individual potential.

Therefore, should we stress knowledge-out-of-context rather than knowledge-in-action? That is, should we ignore other ideas and methods of education that does not conform to the traditional method? In this light, Applebee (1996, p. 43) explains:

> Knowledge-in-action is knowledge that is situated within tradition: if schools are to enable an individual to gain such knowledge, then we must consider how their entry into such traditions can best be facilitated. As students learn to act within the curricular domain, they simultaneously learn both the content and the tacit, socially constituted

conventions that give shape and structure to the larger realms of discourse – they develop the knowledge-in-action that is the living tradition of discourse.

In the ultimate analysis and "in such a system, students are taught about the traditions of the past, and not how to enter into and participate in those [multicultural and educational things] of the present and future" (Applebee, 1996, p. 3). From a purely pragmatic point of view, then, and as Egan (1991, p. 3) suggests, "these ideas have rolled together over the centuries into our currently dominant conception of education. There are just so many variants that one can play with so few ideas before terminal staleness sets in, and matters are made worse by most people's unawareness of the fundamental ideas that shape their thinking about education."

The question that remains is: Can teachers of students in college "shape and present material to students so that it will be meaningful and imaginatively engaging and . . . also stimulate and develop their Philosophic understanding" (Egan, 1991, p. 263)? As Freire (1972, pp. 72-73) has written,

> the point of departure must always be with men [and women] in the 'here and now,' which constitutes the situation within which they are submerged, from which they intervene. Only by starting from this situation – which determines their state not as fated and unalterable, but merely as limiting – and therefore challenging.

After all, and most critically important, "The goals of higher education are to provide students with skills and knowledge that will enable them to be successful in their chosen careers, have an understanding of the human experience, appreciate the aesthetic nature of that experience, and have an intellectual foundation conducive to lifelong learning in the years ahead" (Kent M. and John H. Brudney, 1998, p. 1).

We must, therefore, understand that by providing these new explanations, or opening up the university to other cultural and diverse educational ideas, we will only enrich and 'empower' the student.

In *The Closing of the American Mind*, Bloom (1987, p. 43) made it abundantly clear that our first educational challenge is to "resuscitate those phenomena so that we may again have a world to which we can put our questions and be able to philosophize." Similarly, what Dr. Carter Woodson (1933 and 1969, p. 145) in his famous book, *The Mis-education*

Of the Negro , pointed out in 1933 is as relevant today as it was when he first wrote it: "can [we also] expect teachers to revolutionize the community?" Woodson (1933 and 1969, p. 145), in earnest, goes on, "Indeed we must expect this very thing. The educational system of a country is worthless unless it accomplishes this task. Men of scholarship and consequently of prophetic insight must show us the right and lead us into the light which shines brighter and brighter."

Moreover, any attempt to maintain Black universities, as well as ethnic study programs in the curriculum at major White universities in the United States will continue to be confronted with any number of intractable problems. For example, will the elimination of preferences for minorities at white universities be a death knell for blacks wanting to attend the colleges of their choice? Will there be equal participation? Or "is it in society's interest to have a state-supported institution that excludes people of color based on grades and aptitude tests" (Jones, 1998, p. 28)?

Furthermore, black students at American Universities should definitely be taught in the traditional method in the Eurocentric mold, but the students should also be exposed to different types of curriculums and the larger world – that is, they must be made aware of all the certain complexities in Higher Education – no matter the circumstances and perceived difficulties.

In an increasingly debilitating, convoluted and ambiguous educational system (like the one that exists even today), there must be an emphasis on teaching different types of college curricula, otherwise we are doomed to the traditional status quo. If colleges and universities are to continue to exist into two separate systems of higher education, they should never racially isolate students from people of different racial and cultural backgrounds, with different, diverse, unique and educational points of view.

Additionally, Jones (1998, p. 28) writes that:

We can also keep hope alive by helping European Americans better understand how a diverse education and work environments benefits all of us. We are a multicultural society, and our educational institutions have to do a better job of preparing people for participation in our increasingly complex and diverse world.

In this way, Black and White students can learn important instructional and learning strategies. And through altruism and philosophy, especially in relation to social customs, higher learning, literature and politics, as well as teaching about the different cultures of racial and ethnic groups, while fighting against narcissism, we can improve our depreciating education and the world.

References

Applebee, Arthur N. 1996. *Curriculum As Conversation: Transforming Traditions of Teaching and Learning*. Chicago: The University of Chicago Press.

Bloom, Allan. 1987. *The Closing of the American Mind*. New York: Simon and Schuster, Inc.

Brudney, John H., and Kent M. 1998. *Critical Thinking and American Government*. Forth Worth, Texas: Harcourt Brace and Company.

Egan, Kieran. 1991. *The Educated Mind: How Cognitive Tools Shape Our Understanding*. Chicago: The University of Chicago Press.

Freire, Paulo. 1972. *Pedagogy of the Oppressed*. New York: Herder and Herder New York.

Gwynne, S.C. 1997, June. "Back to the Future." *Time Magazine*.

Jones, Terry. 1998, July-August. "Life After Proposition 209: Affirmative Action May Be Dying, But the Dream Lives On." *Academe*. Vol. 84 No. 4, p. 28.

Levine, Lawrence W. 1996. *The Opening of the American Mind: Canons, Culture, and History*. Boston, Massachusetts: Beacon Press.

Neustadt, R. E., and Ernest R. May. 1986. *Thinking In Time: The Uses of History for Decision Makers*. New York: The Free Press.

Roebuck, J. B., and Murty, K.S. 1993. *Historically Black Colleges and Universities: Their Place in American Higher Education*. Westport, Connecticut: Praeger.

Woodson, Carter G. 1933 and 1969. *Mis-education of the Negro*. Washington, D.C.: The Associated Publishers, Inc.

Chapter Two

ൠൽ

Clash of the Black Titans: W. E. B. DuBois and Booker T. Washington

Part I

W hen I began this chapter, I assumed that *everything* had been written about the tempestuous, controversial and tenuous relationship between William Edward Burghardt DuBois and Booker Taliaferro Washington. Indeed, it is not my purpose here to describe in detail, as others have done, the complex historical situations and relations that existed between the two men.

But my research led me in several different directions, especially about what these two titans stood for. W. E. B. DuBois, who studied at predominantly black Fisk University, and the University of Berlin, was known primarily for being the first black man to attain his Ph.D. from Harvard, and as one of the cofounders of the National Association for the Advancement of Colored People (NAACP), and a supporter of racial equality. Essentially, DuBois, an eminent historian and scholar of Black American intellectual life, was uncompromising and thought that African Americans had every right to achieve not only economic equality, but also parity in politics, as well as in social and economic areas. Toward this end, DuBois believed in using the crème de la crème of black intellectuals, men and women with the vision and foresight, as well as the intellectual curiosity and accomplishments to move the race forward through academic preparation.   And unlike Washington, DuBois also believed and understood that:

> Integration alone could not solve the persistent, daunting educational and emotional problems of many urban and rural black students, problems that were the direct result of poverty and continuing racism (Chamber 1993, p. 185).

Booker T. Washington was the son of a female slave and white slave master, who put himself through school (Hampton Institute in Virginia, in particular) shortly after the Civil War by working in the Virginia coal mines and other odd jobs. Later, he went on to Alabama to start a school for blacks in 1880. And it is clear that without Washington's guidance, business acumen and leadership, Tuskegee Institute (later named Tuskegee University), probably never would have become one of the leading black educational institutions in the United States. Unfortunately, Washington's emphasis on industrial training for blacks as a way of achieving economic independence put him dead center of the controversy with black intellectuals who thought of his proposed policies as outrageous, disingenuous, and going against the grain.

Yes, Washington was condemned by many public black intellectuals of that day, but he was acclaimed by most common black folk and many whites as a great moral leader. Washington (1995, p. 1), however, "absorbed an educational philosophy that emphasized the practical training of African Americans in traditional industrial and agricultural occupations."

Unfortunately, Washington's dream for Blacks in America was not in *sync* with the direction America was taking during that period of our history toward justice and equality – that is, for African Americans. According to William L. Andrews in the introduction to the Oxford University Press edition of *Up From Slavery*, Washington (1995, p. xx) "was not opposed to higher education for African Americans, he just believed that the majority were more in need of vocational training."

Washington's reaction to the political and socioeconomic struggle was never objective, as he raised difficult questions about political oppositions, but colored by the fact that he thought most blacks (not so long out of bondage) could not reasonably formulate ideas on the complex issues of their embattled predicament. One got the impression (from Washington) that poor black people in America should be treated as impressionable children, not the intellectual equals of whites.

DuBois wanted to, in no uncertain terms, make all Americans aware of the evils of institutional racism and discrimination, whereas Washington implied that such evils were not really so bad or consistent for blacks who subordinated themselves, or acquiesced to the dominant society. On the other hand, DuBois confronted the powerful Eurocentric traditions of Education, culture, language, sociology, and politics (head-on), and came to terms with them with his brilliant and prolific scholarship and writings. In fact, through his writings and example, DuBois helped to place the new black or African *intelligentsia* in the forefront of America's cultural mainstream in this period of rising black political and equality consciousness. Indeed, DuBois was a civil rights activist in the finest traditions, as he tried to answer or define the issues of black-liberal education in a totally segregated world at that particular time.

In that sense, DuBois was an educational innovator, a true renaissance man and (racial) modernist in how he approached and presented black thought and *aesthetics*. Moreover, DuBois never eluded definitions of himself, like being a first-rate black scholar. However, the tenets of critical and constructive *pedagogy* presented by DuBois were not often embraced, especially by his enemies. In essence, DuBois was no sympathizer for those against the equality of blacks with whites like Washington.

Even more important, "W. E. B. DuBois," according to Professor Leon F. Litwack (1996, p. 16), "thought a scholarly study of the history of the black experience in the United States might help to undermine racism and raise the historical consciousness of both white and black Americans. But . . . DuBois [did not warrant] much attention [by whites] in a nation which embraced so passionately its racial and historical myths. . . ." In other words, Washington's sphere of influence during the time of his later life was greater than DuBois. Which in essence meant that an overwhelming number of white Americans thought Booker T. Washington was good for race-relations, but not the radical or revolutionary DuBois. But DuBois's vision of the trends in society, especially about the rights of blacks, of the triumph of equality over discrimination and racism, and of the terrible state of repression over blacks throughout the United States, is now generally recognized as relevant and auspicious even to the modern, multi-racial and diversed world.

DuBois, of course, vehemently disagreed with Washington's thoughts for gradual racial progress and his program of accommodation, as "he favored immediate social and political integration and the higher education of a talented tenth of the black population" (Bennett 1993, p. 333). Blacks can learn, DuBois insisted

Part II

About this period of time, Professor Henry Louis Gates (1996, p. 130), Chairman of the Department of Afro-American Studies at Harvard University, has accurately reported:

> DuBois felt, rightly, that Negro Americans were under siege, aided and abetted, wittingly or unwittingly, by Booker T. Washington and his followers, who, DuBois felt, were all too eager to further their own agendas by taking a set of ideological positions which reinforced the larger society's apparent tendency to disenfranchise the Negro and reverse the gains of reconstruction.

Although it may have seemed incongruous for DuBois to be jealous of Washington, he did not like the idea that the "Wizard of Tuskegee" thought he spoke for all blacks in the United States. DuBois did not want us to believe that his attack or motives were those of an opportunist criticizing a less educated black man; but contemporary readers perhaps might sense that DuBois, too, craved publicity because of the confrontation, as did Washington. And as the editor of *The Crisis* (the national magazine of the NAACP), DuBois had a profound effect on the lives of many African Americans. Sociologists Dan S. Green and Edwin Driver (1978, p. 22) have written:

> The effect of DuBois and *The Crisis* on black America during the twenty-four years that he served as editor was immense. *The Crisis* was the first general publication and, at that time, the only national publication written by a black for black consumption. Dubois inspired over a generation of black Americans with his brilliant editorials, informed them of current events of interest to blacks, and regularly published the work of aspiring young black writers. *The Crisis* was the only publication repeatedly and strongly winging and clamoring for civil rights.

Furthermore, as I proceeded to investigate the various accounts and serious disagreement among these two legends (DuBois and Washington), I discovered that the relationship was not so cut and dry, or quite what has been reported by historians. For example, Green and Driver (1978, p. 18) contend, "DuBois was not actively or publicly anti-Washington. He only argued against those parts of his program which were antithetical to his own. He had long admired Washington's accomplishments and agreed with his ideas of black nationalism and self help." DuBois did indeed acknowledge the singular importance of Washington's influence and intuitive leadership as an educator. And DuBois (1961, pp. 43-44) later explained tactfully to others and in his famous book, *The Souls of Black Folk* in 1903:

> [Washington] . . . has gained unquestioning followers, his work has wonderfully prospered, his friends are legion, and his enemies are confounded. Today he stands as the one recognized spokesman of his ten million fellows, and one of the most notable figures in a nation of seventy millions. One hesitates, therefore, to criticize a life which, beginning with so little, has done so much.

DuBois also admitted the astounding success of Washington principally among poor and illiterate blacks who desired an education of some sort. But one might rightly add that there were more uneducated blacks in many states in America during the period shortly after the Civil War. Of course, black people have always been excluded in past American histories, and the political mainstream, and viewed as inconsequential. Furthermore, DuBois could never accept the inferior position or status assigned to black Americans, and especially those individuals who would contribute or sustain the fight against black repression, separatism, oppression and disfranchisement.

Although neither man's eyes were closed to the deplorable plight and condition of black people in the South and elsewhere, Washington's philosophy was more in line with the old southern point of view, or he followed the official line or positions of most white Americans: that civil rights activists and leaders, demanding equality and desegregation, were part of the larger problem in terms of race relations.

Washington's attacks were usually directed against those who disagreed with his approach toward education, his leadership style, and *modus operandi*. And as William L. Andrews also pointed out, "Washington felt no compunction about using underhanded means,

including paid spies and informants, to subvert those whom he saw as
rivals or enemies in the African American leadership of his day" (Washington 1995, p. xxii). Washington resisted the civil and equal rights
movements in the nation, as he had no desire to *publicly* promote the
fundamental rights of blacks, and was critical of the many black leaders
of that day, like DuBois, whom he referred to as an agitator. He also
deplored the rhetoric of desegregation and racial antagonism. Perhaps
Washington (made the mistake of) demanding total loyalty and devotion
from those rebellious black intellectuals and educators he did not even
know.

Washington's life was full of triumphs and tragic contradictions. He
was loved and hated simultaneously and to excess in some quarters, and
clearly his life was damaged by those who disagreed and challenged him.
Washington recognized that the black leaders who opposed him were
energized by the growing forces of DuBois and the civil rights movement.
And many even thought of him as *Uncle Tomish*.

This does not mean, however, that Washington's feelings were
motivated by absolute malice toward DuBois and other black scholars.
Indeed, Washington realized that his disgust and dislike for black leaders
who did not see eye-to-eye or things his way was largely rooted, perhaps,
in his own ambitions and a stubborn need to be accepted by everyone and
for his own self-justification and edification. Or perhaps Washington
thought that DuBois and other black radicals or upstarts wanted *equality*
for nefarious purposes.

Part III

W. E. B. DuBois, of course, challenged the basic premises of
segregation and the subordination of blacks, and this became the bone of
contention with Washington. Washington, moreover, actually courted
the approval of the black community. Unfortunately, he was not dis-
passionate in his beliefs and analysis of other despised leaders. Which
begs the question: Was Washington jealous of them making inroads with
the black population at large? Or was he frustrated with these new black
and vocal leaders trying to usurp the authority and leadership role he
carefully cultivated and perhaps thought he deserved and maintained in
the black community of the time?

In the final analysis, and unlike many black intellectuals at the time,
Washington viewed American perspectives on race relations with

suspicion, mistrust and with apprehension. But DuBois embodied a new attitude that was unprecedented, irreversible and would grow. Black activists idolized DuBois. And according to distinguished black historian Benjamin Quarles (1969, p. 173) "College-trained Negroes had a more direct response to DuBois' esteem for them: many of them joined him in the anti-Washington movement." In this sense, there is no doubt that Washington suffered intense anguish over not being embraced by the majority of black students and black intellectuals.

DuBois, nonetheless, had high praise and admiration for Washington, recognizing that he was after all an African American leader to be reckoned with. During the time of his life, Washington was well known as "the Wizard of Tuskegee" by most African Americans who knew him; but he wanted to be known as well, by all concerned and like-minded white Americans and supporters as the primary black leader who could up-lift the black race and at the same time, keep them humble, subservient and perhaps, complacently in line. Washington, of course, would become the only black leader some white Americans believed in and trusted as far as the struggle for education in the black community was concerned.

While many blacks were able to understand DuBois' rejection of Washington's moderate, traditionalist-conservative or accommodationist approach to race relation, they were still left to ponder the rationalization of his staunch alliance with Southern whites who helped or allowed him to build Tuskegee Institute, formerly a poor industrial school in Tuskegee, Alabama, and the surrounding black community.

Some scholars stressed that there was an unmistakable rivalry between the two men, as both black leaders were fighting for the heart, soul and intellectual minds of blacks in America. Indeed, many scholars and historians have noted and commented on this bitter hostility. However, one must be fully cognizant that outside of both of these men's intellectual lives, certain scholars are too narrowly focused to acknowledge the untenable or true situation that actually existed between Washington and DuBois. For example, Professors Mary Frances Berry and John W. Blassingame (1982, p. 97) wrote that Washington was "an intimate friend of W. E. B. DuBois and saw no conflict between the ideologies of the two men, [as they] often conferred at his home."

Nonetheless, the squabble between DuBois and Washington was real, not imagined. Indeed, there was something of almost biblical proportions about the confrontation between the two black leaders. As Washington questioned the authenticity of W. E. B. DuBois, undoubtedly the most brilliant black scholar of his time, who became a revered leader of the civil rights movement, DuBois questioned Washington's leadership itself. The late Professor Benjamin Quarles (1969, p. 172) wrote:

> Impressed by the scholarly attainments of DuBois, Washington had at first sought to enlist him as a lieutenant, but DuBois' ambition and abilities, plus his haughtiness, made him unsuitable as a subordinate. Possibly it was this effort to assume leadership among Negroes that led DuBois to attack Washington's policies. But conviction also played a role, for by 1903 he had come to the conclusion that Washington was "leading the way backward."

Washington, of course, believed in predestination and thought blacks should accept their subordinate role in America and not agitate (as suggested by militant black intellectuals like DuBois) for racial, social justice, political rights and equality in all aspects of our country. In characterizing DuBois, Washington contended that the irreverent insights of such a brilliant mind or public intellectual, however important in general significance, did not necessarily make for desired and righteous change. Still the degree of black Americans wanting immediate power and influence in their day-to-day lives worried Washington to no end.

Washington, of course, was a contemporary of DuBois, who can be thought of as a radical or visionary himself; however, according to Franklin and Moss (1994, p. 274), DuBois "especially denounced the manner in which Washington deprecated [black] institutions of higher learning," because they ultimately served as the fertile ground upon which seeds of training, education and learning were planted. Therefore, in this sense, it must be understood that "DuBois also charged Washington with being hostile to Negro liberal arts colleges and their graduates" (Quarles, 1969, p. 73). More importantly, DuBois disassociated himself from Washington's subservient attitude and politics about life for African Americans, and "tacit acceptance of the alleged inferiority of the Negro" (Quarles 1969, p. 173). Although both men spoke out eloquently about the racial problems in the United States, prominent black scholars wantonly criticized Washington for putting the status quo and conservative ideology ahead of social equality. Washington focused on education, economic parity, and hard, menial work. And as it has been noted, critics of Washington have long recognized his status and importance, but they hated his shameful "bowing and scraping" for hand-outs or financing from whites, while preaching self-reliance.

Booker T. Washington essentially believed as Harvard Professor William Julius Wilson (1996, p. 204) does – that is, concerning the education of blacks that was most acceptable to whites during that time – when he wrote:

> Programs that enable[d] blacks to take advantage of opportunities, such as race-targeted early education programs and job training, [were] less likely to be "perceived as challenging the values of individualism and the work ethic." In other words, compensatory or opportunity-enhancing affirmative action programs [were] supported because they reinforce[d] the belief that the allocation of jobs and economic rewards should be based on individual effort, training, and talent.

In other words, Washington emphasized industrial, agricultural education, trades and school-teaching over book-learning. Washington (1995, p. xxi) in fact became "the most influential black champion of the idea of vocational and technical education for African Americans in the South." For some American intellectuals and educated blacks, Washington's political, economic and social policies were an insult to their collective intelligence and the learning abilities of the race everywhere. And still for others, Washington became the most despised or unappreciated black man or leader in America, as "It was the Washington school's contention that the Negro must crawl before he could walk, that industrial education was more necessary than academic learning and that compromise on suffrage and equal rights might" better serve African Americans (Hughes and *et al* 1995, p. 244).

Part IV

Of course, Washington knew of the unwritten policy between blacks and whites – that is, that they wouldn't or shouldn't cross the line or dominant group's path, and that blacks should accept the political status quo for their own good. But Washington freely acknowledged the struggle among the races. So as painful as it was, the often reported squabble between DuBois and Washington on these issues truly existed. But it was a more complex relationship that involved negative as well as positive factors. According to historian Lerone Bennett (1993, p. 332), "The antagonism between [the DuBois and Washington factions] is generally and inaccurately described as a struggle over industrial education vs.

higher education. But the core of the problem lay deeper than this. The whole controversy turned on leadership, not trades; on power, not education" (Bennett 1993, p. 332).

Question: Was Washington's posturing just a play to gain the good graces of white benefactors and mainly financial support for Tuskegee Institute and other important projects? Based on Washington's personal papers, it has been brought to light that:

> Although Washington gave whites the impression that he was an accommodator of segregation, he secretly financed and directed several court suits against various kinds of discrimination in the South, including disenfranchisement and segregation in railroad facilities (Washington 1995, p. xxii).

Professor of history at George Mason University, Jeffrey C. Stewart (1996, pp. 126-127) explained it this way:

> Despite his public disavowal of Black political resistance and his obsequious manner of presenting himself to white people, Booker T. Washington actually worked behind the scenes to defend African American political and social rights. In 1898, for example, he not only asked the Louisiana legislature to ensure that the understanding clause and other restrictions on voting would be applied fairly, but he also lent his financial support to legal challenges to the constitutionality of Louisiana's grandfather clause. Secretly he financially supported efforts to end racial discrimination of Pullman cars in southern states. He also provided money to lawyers seeking to overturn statutes in Texas and Alabama that excluded African Americans from participation on juries. Washington did all of this secretly and quietly, usually through organizations like the Afro-American Council, to avoid alerting whites that he was working against segregation and disfranchisement.

Perhaps Washington was misunderstood, and his opinions about politics and economics for blacks were taken out of context. His methods were definitely questionable. Or perhaps DuBois and the community of black scholars did not realize how pervasive or far-reaching Washington's political skills were with which he dealt with white Americans to get what he wanted. After all, one of the most famous white philanthropists at that time, Andrew Carnegie was taken-in, or influenced by the considerable charm of Washington, as he once gave the black leader

$150,000 for personal speaking engagements and contributed an astonishing sum (for the time) of $600,000 to Tuskegee Institute (Harlan 1983, p. 135). Therefore, we should not be fooled by Washington's so-called meekness and political naivete.

Another like-minded philanthropist, Julius Rosenwald, a white, American Jew, who believed in giving generously of his "fortune for the welfare of others" was also impressed by Booker T. Washington's dynamic educational track record. In fact, "inspired and assisted by Washington," Rosenwald:

> Financed the construction of new schools and in some cases provided funds for their maintenance. His [Rosenwald's] activity started slowly, in the area near Tuskegee, Alabama, but later expanded into all the Southern states. By 1931, 20 years after he started, he had financed 5,295 school buildings. He had contributed, mainly but not entirely for the schools, about $650 million in present purchasing power.

> In all his giving, [moreover], Rosenwald insisted that the local government assume responsibility for the operation of the schools once they were completed. That was sometimes difficult to achieve. "Local government" meant the white establishment, which was often reluctant to commit itself to spending for the education of blacks, or fearful of the hostility of bigots in their community. But enough whites of courage and humanity were found to permit the program to succeed. In at least one case all preparations for constructing the school had to be made surreptitiously, so that the building could be quickly erected before the Ku Klux Klan could interfere (Stein 1998, p. A22).

Nonetheless, and despite his good works, DuBois criticized Washington in his famous essay, "Of Mr. Booker T. Washington and Others," in *The Souls of Black Folk*, which, according to Distinguished Professor of history at the University of Maryland, Louis R. Harlan (1983, pp. 50-51) "was the most persuasive intellectual critique ever written of Washington's racial strategy – both his industrial education and accommodationism." DuBois scathingly wrote:

> 1. [Washington] is striving nobly to make Negro artisans businessmen and property-owners; but it is utterly impossible, under modern competitive methods, for workingmen and property-owners to defend their rights and exist without the right of suffrage.

2. [Washington] insists on thrift and self-respect, but at the same time counsels a silent submission to civic inferiority such as is bound to sap the manhood of any race in the long run.

3. [Washington] advocates common-school and industrial training, and depreciates institutions of higher learning; but neither the Negro common-schools, not Tuskegee itself, could remain open a day were it not for teachers trained in Negro colleges, or trained by their graduates (DuBois 1961, p. 49).

These criticisms about Washington, outlined by DuBois, were the most prominent social, economic and educational issues of that day. But as one can perhaps determine from the above passages, DuBois was ideologized, as was Washington. According to Professor Kenneth W. Warren (1993, p. 117), however, "the path of Booker T. Washington was not the proper path for black America." Nor did Washington reflect the widespread sentiment among African-Americans for a level playing field in jobs and educational opportunities. This begs a more pertinent question: Why? In response, we could essentially say, DuBois "came to represent the future, and Washington the past" (Harlan 1983, p. 360). Warren goes on to write that DuBois had "an apt image of the potential of black America if it pursued political and intellectual equality and of the dangers it faced if black folk accepted the program of Washington," (Warren 1993, p. 117) which taught or advocated the inverse of this (uplifting) philosophy.

Interestingly enough, Washington "publicly branded DuBois a "radical" and a racial agitator," (Green and Driver 1978, p. 19) but many of his enemies denounced his brand of tired leadership. DuBois wanted to create (on the other hand) a new image of the Negro (or Blacks), which departed considerably from Washington's passive stance or view, but Washington often thought of DuBois' particular rhetoric and political philosophy as subversive. Professor Arnold Rampersad (1990, p. 64) has insightfully written, "DuBois would soon come to view Washington as a political boss of substantial and ruthless power, acting as a broker between the black and white worlds; he in turn would be perceived by Washington as a menace to his carefully established and exquisitely maintained influence."

What is surprising, furthermore, is that there was a notable disparity between the two men, especially in terms of ideologies. Harlan (1983, p. 51) summarizes significant aspects of these differences when he wrote:

The burden of DuBois' rejection of Washington was that his materialism and his compromises with white tyranny denied blacks their right to dream, to aspire, to master the world around them. The very restraint with which DuBois presented his case, conceding Washington's genuine fostering of black self-help and acknowledging that he often opposed racial injustice in his own way, rendered DuBois's arguments more persuasive. . . .

DuBois believed that Washington was in collusion with Southern whites, which he thought would eventually hurt blacks. But the genesis of the disagreement or fall-out between Washington and DuBois started with Washington's controversial speech at Atlanta, which generated much divisiveness, and ill feelings. Indeed, this "Atlanta compromise" speech proved to be sensational, for it made Washington a national celebrity and affirmed what white wanted to hear about the acquiescence and accommodation of black people in the United States. Whites, of course, were often pleased by Washington's self-reliance rhetoric and highly praised his thoughts and ideas about the levels of education blacks should receive. But he was righteously damned by black leaders of the time. The famous speech at Atlanta, given humbly by Washington, however, allowed him to continue receiving charity and needed finances for the construction of new school buildings in and around Tuskegee, Alabama. However, this event finished off the relations the two men had. Hence, the conflict was also centered on their relationship, but "it was partly due to Booker T. Washington's stress on industrial rather than liberal arts education that the controversy developed between his followers and those of W. E. B. DuBois" (Hughes 1995, p. 248).

Furthermore, Washington's modest proposal or speech at Atlanta created a stir and "a philosophical breach" between these two black leaders that "soon widened over the years" (Hughes 1995, p. 244). To say the least, it drove a permanent wedge between them. Middle and upper-class African-Americans read about Washington's statements as being in support of some kind of new slavery or servitude. And in a sense, Washington provided whites with ideological ammunition for their fight against blacks achieving any kind of equality and those rights supposedly guaranteed by the United States Constitution and Bill of Rights. Others would also disagree with Washington's analysis of the racial situation. DuBois, on the other hand, believed and argued persuasively that intellectual differences among blacks and whites were only slight, and due primarily to social and environmental factors. What is especially significant during this time (the early 1900s) was the fledgling civil rights movement.   In fact, DuBois's radical or arguably extremist position concerning blacks achieving equal rights with whites became a central tenet of the civil rights movement that took its inspiration from the black church and black, college-trained men and women. Prior to the creation of the National Association for the Advancement of Colored People (NAACP), and before that, the Niagara Movement, which began in 1905, DuBois and Washington at least talked, or communicated. But afterward, they – or rather both of them – quietly divorced themselves – philosophically and ideologically – from each other.

According to Green and Driver (1978, pp. 18-19), "The Niagara Movement is significant in American history and in the life of DuBois in that it foreshadowed future civil rights organizations [like the NAACP and CORE] and provided blacks a choice between the melioristic and conservative program of Washington and the more radical and forceful policy of legal protest espoused by DuBois and his followers."   The Niagara Movement was also a way of challenging Jim Crowism and the violation of the rights of black Americans. About the importance of the movement, and perhaps the beginning of the ideological differences between Washington and DuBois, Quarles (1969, p. 173) had this to say:

> In the summer of 1905 DuBois officially launched his own movement at a meeting held at Niagara Falls, Canada, which was attended by twenty-nine members of the Talented Tenth from thirteen states and the District of Columbia. Avoiding any open criticism of Booker T. Washington, the conferees drew up a manifesto which called for freedom of speech and of the press, the abolition of discrimination based on race or color, and a recognition of the principles of human brotherhood. The delegates proclaimed that until they got the rights belonging to free-born Americans, they would never cease to protest. . . .

Washington, nevertheless, passionately believed that what could not be achieved for blacks through vocational education, *guile* and diplomacy perhaps could. In this sense, DuBois recognized Washington's pragmatic brilliance. But the criticisms leveled at Washington during his later life dealt mainly with his meliorism and unwillingness to accept other ways of approaching or attacking the problems of race and the deplorable condition of the blacks of his time (other than his own methods). According to Professor Asafa Jalata (1995, p. 160), for example, Washington, "until his death in 1915, limited the effectiveness of the NAACP and militant black intellectuals because of his challenge to protest and political action," and because of his access to the dominant culture's power and wealth.

Moreover, though Washington at times waffled on the question of whether there could be two black leaders at the same time, DuBois realized the irony. Washington's accomplishments, notwithstanding the propitious speech he made at Atlanta, were tremendous. Consider these remarks by Franklin and Moss (1994, pp. 276-277):

> Despite the fact that there were blacks who vigorously opposed Washington's leadership and that there were some valid exceptions to his program for the salvation of his people, he was unquestionably the central figure – the dominant personality – in the history of African Americans until his death in 1915.

Part V

It should be admitted that DuBois's formidable intellect and experiences contrasted sharply with Washington's street smarts. And despite the hostility and suspicions, both men were powerful and important voices for the plight of African-Americans in the United States without equal during their time. Many scholars have noted parallels between DuBois and Washington, but we must ask what role can understanding these two giants play in transforming the lives of black Americans today? Moreover, what can one say about the racialism and divisiveness that existed during the times of DuBois and Washington, and continue to exist in the predominantly black and white communities, the academic realm and halls of higher education?

One of the most serious problems confronted by scholars and historians is that only some things can be understood because of the context of their particular time and place. Nevertheless I believe in trying to understand what meaning and (educational) implications DuBois and Washington may have for us in the future.

The discordance between the two men is similar to the on-going conflict and debate of black conservatives versus black liberals in our society today, because both groups want different things – or suggest opposing ways – to solve our various racial and political exigencies. Conservative blacks in the academy would acquiesce to the ruling or dominant elite – or those who control and rule this nation.   Whereas black liberals and proactive academics would propose such novel measures as using or establishing government programs that would educate all minorities in educational endeavors, including the hard sciences and mathematics.

The question we must seriously ask is: Would such an approach be for the greater good of our society? In the final analysis, we can all learn from the lives, exploits and splendid stories of DuBois and Washington. Nevertheless, there still seems to be a small elite group of educated blacks within and outside the academia – as it was in the past – that continue to clash with each other, and divide blacks in the diaspora over education.

Part VI

DuBois and Washington were intellectual giants (or heavy-weights) in America's academic world, though from totally different backgrounds and levels of education. Their words and writings, however, presented the political commentary about blacks of the day. For example, if there is any book that defined the aspirations of many illiterate and uneducated blacks during the time of Washington's life, *Up From Slavery* filled that void. *Up From Slavery* also revealed the impasse in which Washington found himself with regard to the black situation. Not altogether surprisingly, DuBois's life work has left a legacy of brilliant scholarship in African-American history, and has been widely acknowledged as the very best of academic writing from learned institutions across America.

Moreover, the emphasis that both DuBois and Washington placed on education was significant in itself, as they tried to educate young blacks, however different they were in their approaches. DuBois, I believe, rightly attacked (and explicitly rejected) Booker T. Washington's call for the education of blacks in vocational areas to achieve economic and social equality. However, Herbert Stein (1998, p. A22), an American Enterprise Institute fellow has ventured, "Washington was the country's leading proponent of the idea that education was the road not only to economic advancement for blacks but also to political and social advancement." Washington spent much of the rest of his time before he died expanding Tuskegee and writing down what he thought about the place of blacks in the world and America.   "In his own time," as Professor Kennell Jackson

(1996, p. 218) tells us, Washington "was beloved by many Blacks, admired by whites, and opposed mightily by Black intellectuals. Decades after his death, he is still controversial. Yet few Black debates have escaped his imprint." Nonetheless, Washington was both canonized and demonized upon death.

Paradoxically, William Edward Burghardt DuBois remained controversial throughout his life, admired or despised for his liberal and radical views, his elitism and quiet, intellectual dignity. DuBois never relented in his criticism of American racism. The FBI even thought of DuBois as a national threat and had an extensive dossier on his comings and goings. For example, citing from an FBI file in 1942 is the following:

> Subject [is] presently professor at Atlanta University, Atlanta, Georgia. He received his higher education at Harvard, traveled in Europe, and studied in Berlin. Subject is poet and former editor of *Crisis* magazine, a publication sponsored by the N. A. A. C. P. He now writes a column in the *Amsterdam New York Star News*. His writings indicate him to be a socialist. However, he has been called a communist and at the same time criticized by the Communist Party. Subject favors equality between the white and colored races. No evidence of subversive activity in New York (O'Reilly 1994, p. 85).

DuBois, a civil rights leader and extraordinary scholar, until the end, never shied away from exploring uncomfortable subjects and racial issues. Nor did he make concessions to his own convictions. He lived a long life, joining the Communist Party in 1961, and moved to Ghana (in Africa) where he died (and was buried) in 1963 at the age of ninety-one.

It is, of course, instructive to compare these two black leaders; but finally, can we ever truly understand the underlying reasons for the irreconcilable conflict between DuBois and Washington? The point here is both of these two heroes were concerned with the welfare of blacks and Africans within and outside the United States, and wanted blacks to succeed no matter the consequences, price or circumstances. The central fact is that even though they were diametrically opposed to each other, they both made ground-breaking and enormous contributions to the important canon of African-American aesthetics, our intellectual foundation, and added to the great public debate of their time.

References

Bennett, Lerone, Jr. 1993. *Before The Mayflower: A History of Black America*. New York: Penguin Books.

Berry, Mary Frances and Blassingame, John. 1982. *Long Memory: The Black Experience in America*. New York: Oxford University Press.

Chamber, Julius L. 1993. "Brown v Board of Education." *Race in America: The Struggle for Equality*, edited by Herbert Hill and James E. Jones, Jr. Madison, Wisconsin: The University of Wisconsin Press.

DuBois, Burghardt, W. E. 1961. *The Souls of Black Folk*. Greenwich, Connecticut: Fawcett Publications, Inc.

Franklin, John Hope, and Moss, Alfred, A. Jr. 1994. *From Slavery To Freedom: A History Of African Americans*. New York: McGraw-Hill, Inc.

Green, Dan S. and Driver, Edwin D., Editors. 1978. *W. E. B. DuBois: On Sociology and the Black Community*. Chicago: The University of Chicago Press.

Harlan, Zouis R. 1983. *Booker T. Washington: The Wizard of Tuskegee 1901-1915*. New York: Oxford University Press.

Hughes, Langston, Meltzer, Milton, Lincoln, Eric C., Spencer, Michael Jon. 1995. *A Pictorial History of African Americans*. 6th Edition. New York: Crown Publishers, Inc.

Jackson, Kennell. 1996. *America Is Me: 170 Fresh Questions and Answers On Black American History*. New York: Harper Collins.

Jalata, Asafa. 1995. "African American Nationalism, Development, and Afrocentricity: Implications for the Twenty-First Century," in *Molefi Kete Asante and Afrocentricity: In Praise and in Criticism*, edited by Dhyana Ziegler. Nashville, Tennessee: James Winston Publishing Company, Inc.

Litwack, Leon F. 1996. "The Making of A Historian," in *Historians and Race: Autobiography and The Writing of History*. Indianapolis: Indiana University Press.

O'Reilly, Kenneth. 1994. *Black Americans: The FBI Files*, edited by David Gallen. New York: Carroll and Graf Publishers, Inc.

Quarles, Benjamin. 1969. *The Negro in the Making of America*, revised edition. New York: The Macmillan Company.

Rampersad, Arnold. 1990. *The Art and Imagination of W. E. B. DuBois*. New York: Schocken Books.

Stein, Herbert. 1998 Tuesday, February 24. "A Model of Philanthropy." *The Wall Street Journal*.

Steward, Jeffrey C. 1996. *1001 Things Everyone Should Know About African American History*. New York: Doubleday.

Warren, Kenneth W. 1993. *Black and White Strangers: Race and American Literary Realism*. Chicago: The University of Chicago Press.

Washington, Booker T. 1995 edition. *Up From Slavery*. New York: Oxford
    University Press.
Wilson, William Julius. 1996. *When Work Disappears: The World of the New
    Urban Poor*. New York: Alfred A. Knopf.

Chapter Three

ℰℭ

Crisis of the African American Student and the Development of Historically Black Colleges and Universities

Rise of the African American Student

While teaching a graduate course in public policy and personnel administration at a major university in the Southwest, one wide-eyed and curious white student asked me: Why did blacks want their own separate colleges and universities? He went on to clarify himself by stating – erroneously, I might add – that he thought that blacks should not have higher education institutions, because there wasn't really a need. To say the least, I was flabbergasted by the student's lack of knowledge and historical understanding. To say the least, I was shocked by the student's naivete. "Did he not know the real reasons these schools were created in the first place?" I wondered. Apparently not.

At that instant, I also got the impression that most Americans are ignorant about the precarious development of these complex institutions – that is, how and why historically black colleges and universities were created in the first place. Indeed, there is the myth that these schools were created separate and apart from white universities because black people wanted or preferred it that way. This is simply not the case, or nothing could be further from the truth. The reality, of course, was blacks wanted to be educated, but they were not allowed to attend predominantly white universities throughout America. For instance, "as a result of segregation blacks had to go outside the South for professional training" (Berry and Blassingame 1982, p. 286). Moreover, and according to the brilliant black newspaper columnist, DeWayne Wickham (1993, p. 12A), "it was in reaction to the segregation many white Americans once openly demanded that most black educational institutions were created. That's how black colleges got their start."

Furthermore, critics of higher education say that the existence of both predominantly black and white education systems is unjust, redundant (and difficult to maintain) because it places an unfair burden on those black students, (especially those) who must determine where they want to be educated. Some have even said that black colleges and universities are the most troubled sites in education. Some even "argue that putting resources into education to improve the intellectual performance of [black] students from deprived backgrounds is a waste of money" (Stringer and McKie 1996, p. 190).

The education crisis of black students, furthermore, is often cited as the root cause of the poverty and troubles in the inner city as many black colleges struggle to streamline their finances and curriculums. Unfortunately, many black institutions of higher learning offer limited curricular. For example, "most of the black colleges in 1955 still concentrated on teacher training to the virtual exclusion of professional training" (Berry and Blassingame 1982, p. 286). Furthermore, as far as black students are concerned, who often protest the debilitating and deteriorating quality of their education, Neil Postman (1996, pp. 166-167) tells us that:

> American students are well tuned to respond with feeling, critical intelligence, and considerable attention to forms of popular music [like Rap and Rock], but are not prepared to feel or even to experience the music of Haydn, Bach, or Mozart; that is to say, their hearts are closed, or partially closed, to the canon of Western music [and education for that matter].

Moreover, the college student of today, if "left to their own devices, develop no strong intellectual interests and, as a consequence," (Reuben 1996, p. 233) many take classes out of necessity and are only concerned with passing courses with an acceptable grade in order to complete the requirements for graduation. So in this sense, complaints (about our lax education) are not necessarily justified, nor do they deserve, I believe, our immediate support and understanding.

The problem may also be stated or understood in the following way: "black students who are ill-equipped for the work they confront [in college] demand a great deal more time and effort than many faculties originally contemplated" (Manne 1978, p. 192). But do we have the time or can we afford the luxury of allowing blacks in general, the opportunity for an education? Moreover, should our taxes help subsidize the educational studies of black students who gain the privilege of admission to the university? Even more important, should race be taken into account in selecting minority students – with lesser high school credentials – for admissions to college? Or should higher education remain the responsibility of state and local governments, or an entitlement funded by the nation? Indeed, what should be the state and federal role in education?

Unfortunately, some historically black institutions of higher education have lapsed into mediocrity through a combination of a lack of university (state and federal) funding, a decrease in giving by philanthropists, and the democratization of our education system. And this is important to understand because according to Henry G. Manne (1978 p. 192), "The expansion of outside funds [for black colleges and universities in particular] has stopped, and there have actually been cutbacks."

Ultimately, we must ask: If black students are not accepted to certain educational institutions in the United States, will they be denied admission and scholarship opportunities at numerous and highly selective colleges? Furthermore, if racial preference programs are eliminated at most white universities for blacks, will there be a stronger need to establish and maintain separate black colleges and universities? Again, Henry G. Manne (1978, pp. 192-193) writes, "Interest is clearly beginning to wane in special programs for black students, and the next few years will probably witness, under various rationalizations, a return to the standard of scholastic ability as the near-exclusive criterion for admission, other than payment of tuition."

Therefore, will black students be given the same academic opportunities within the context of these vast social and educational changes? What one must also realize.is: Historically black college admissions nationwide still face a revolution in the academic community in terms of enrollment. Indeed, can the gap between black and white universities be bridged by bringing the various political factions, as well as academic cultures, together in America? Professor Walter Gill (1991, p. 45) echoes this sentiment when he stressed:

> By looking at societal change and current trends in education, implications for tomorrow's schools, the curriculum, and instructional strategies can be seen. Some of the educational issues confronting the United States in the 1990s, and educational decisions as they affect nonwhite groups, will be difficult to make given the present mentality of today's governing bodies. An educational maturity on the part of educators, teachers and students will receive the kind of humanistic training and instruction needed for productivity in a pluralistic society.

Furthermore, and albeit unfortunately, many black colleges and universities fail to adapt to a fast-changing world with global markets and the communications revolution. However, these institutions are still regarded as temples of higher education and learning in the black community. Moreover, and most fundamentally, there seems to be a broad consensus that "the [black] colleges have not been successful . . . in convincing the wider society of their merit, largely because of the need to document the somewhat intangible service they do or do not render" (Fleming 1984, p. ix).

The very range of colleges and universities in the United States reflects a complex mix of educational, and cultural issues related to the direction and priorities of African Americans. At their heart is perhaps the central challenge of black American educational life, which is how to survive. Indeed, when predominantly black colleges and universities were established, the question of whether they would continue to exist was never asked. But this is still the crucial question surrounding black institutions of higher learning.

Therefore, are we shortchanging our own future by contemplating the elimination of predominantly black colleges and universities? Or can we create the kind of ethos that are needed in order to sustain and maintain black colleges and universities? After all, and historically, "black colleges have been the primary educators of black Americans. Now, even though most black students [can] choose to go to predominantly white institutions, those who speak for black colleges believe these schools continue to perform a service, chiefly in motivating students" (Fleming, 1984, p. ix). Therefore, we must never underestimate the extent or length black colleges and universities will take or go to survive and protect themselves from peril and ultimate ruin or disintegration.

Equally important, we must also ask: Is racial diversity still important on white American campuses? Perhaps it is as Dinesh D'Souza (1991, p. 228) writes in *Illiberal Education*: "Because [white] universities have exhausted the patience of the most sympathetic advocates of the victim's revolution, the back lash against preferential treatment [for black] and sensitivity education will continue to get worse. . . . Or the worst is yet to come."

In some respects D'Souza's dire prediction has come true in that many learned institutions across America are eliminating programs and so-called preferential treatment for minorities. But what these colleges and universities fail to realize is whether there will be any adversed repercussions in the future. In race-obsessed United States, and with the elimination of Affirmative Action on college campuses, one must ask: Will there be a return to America's colleges and universities to pre-dominantly white and black bastions of separate education? And while the crisis about higher learning deepens, the governments in several states where black schools are represented (or located) are still bickering over whether black institutions of higher education should continue to even exist at all.

What D'Souza and other like-minded and misguided conservatives fail to understand is as Talcott Parsons and Gerald M. Platt (1973, p. 201) remind us:

> The poor and blacks have already changed the content of undergraduate education: witness growing programs and departments in Afro-American studies, Third World studies, courses and programs on women. . . . Such populations will continue to place pressure on faculties to shift the content of courses. In so far as this is accomplished, the materials taught and learned will have new kinds of meaning for the lives of their students. Thus, broadened population inclusion is a subtle form of influence toward the teaching of relevant, applied, practical, ideological, and politically salient topics.

Therefore, what are the basic solutions to America's higher educational crisis, and the problems of black universities in particular? First, we must remember that many of these colleges and universities have a long and rich history of educating and helping blacks become college graduates. And ultimately, they give black students the promise of educational opportunity. Moreover, in order to debate intelligently about the future of historically black colleges and universities, we must not concentrate on the notion of whether they are needed, but we must focus or look instead at the necessity or the merit of the institutions themselves. According to Professor Walter Gill (1991, p. 45):

> As of 1987, African American colleges and universities enroll one [out] of every six African Americans in higher education with graduation rates when compared to white institutions of higher learning. . . . [And] for the most part, white institutions have not been successful in developing comprehensive programs designed to recruit, retain and graduate a more culturally and racially diverse population.

Hence, black colleges and universities are still vitally important to the American educational system and "crucial in producing the Black college-educated middle classes" (Jackson. 1996, p. 186). And alone with religion, black education, in fact, constitutes one of the most important factors in the black community. And predominantly black institutions of higher education are now drawing the country's crème de la crème of black students. We must also recognize that "in the long run impact of Negro scholarship and Negro perceptions on the intellectual life of the university cannot constitute anything but an enrichment. That particular enrichment cannot, however, take place if the Negro scholar withdraws into his own course and segregates himself from the conflict of ideas and the noise of debate which should characterize every university campus" (Tonsor 1978, p. 214). In other words, black intellectuals should not create or invent educational programs, academic disciplines, or courses that alienate or infuriate their academic colleagues, as this could be detrimental to their professional growth and development as legitimate scholars. For example, the new discipline of Afrocentricity has yet to overcome skepticism fueled by opponents of the field. This is not to say that we shouldn't establish new courses or academic disciplines, but after a set period of time or implementation phase, they must be just as precise and rigorous in imparting information to students as already established disciplines.

Staunch conservative and eminent economist and black historian of American socio-economic life, Thomas Sowell (1993, p. x) has written:

> At the college and university level, the intrusion of nonintellectual and anti-intellectual material into the curriculum takes more of an ideological, rather than a psychological, form. New courses, new programs concentrate on leading students to preconceived ideological conclusions, rather than developing the student's ability to analyze issues so as to reach independent conclusions.

American educational issues will dominate the social concerns of blacks in the United States in the future, because, "Today, education is perhaps the most important function of state and local governments. Compulsory school attendance laws and the great expenditures for education both demonstrate our democratic society. It is required in the performance of our most basic public responsibilities, even service in the armed forces. It is the very foundation of good citizenship" (Wexler 1993, p. 275). And if this is so, is it any wonder blacks have wanted to be educated or to at least have the ability to read and write since being brought to the Americas in chains, as slaves?

Historical Development of Black Colleges and Universities

Now it is important to consider the history of black colleges and universities from their earliest development to their present day role as a force for social change for African American or black citizens, especially in terms of education. Historically black universities, like historically white universities stressed educational concerns in their respective communities. But it must be clearly understood that black colleges and universities started or were created from a totally different and unique perspective. Perhaps the growth in these fledgling institutions was driven by the need to educate blacks not so long in chains. Indeed, "the origins of the institutions were modest. The first Black colleges were the result of small donations from missionary groups and the Freedman's Bureau" (Jackson 1996, p. 187). In fact, some of America's leading black institutions were founded by these important missionaries. Moreover, black colleges were established side by side with black churches and black lodges.

"Founded in many cases," according to Lerone Bennett (1988, p. 290), "by far-sighted black men and women, these institutions played a crucial role in redirecting the leadership wave, sending out year after year bands of potential rebels, who were leaven in the lump of black despair." Furthermore, many black leaders, in the past and presently, have graduated from predominantly black universities, and they make up almost the entire educated work force and black middle classes in the United States. Harold Wenglinsky (1998, p. 1), in his path-breaking study of the accomplishments of black institutions, writes:

Behind many of today's prominent Black leaders lies a college education
at Historically Black Colleges and Universities (HBCUs). Famous
graduates of HBCUs include political figures Douglas Wilder, Louis
Sullivan, and Andrew Young, Jr.; writers Toni Morrison and Alice
Walker; opera singer Jessye Norman; and television personalities Oprah
Winfrey and Phylicia Rashad. These HBCU graduates are only the
most recent generation to achieve prominence. Earlier graduating
HBCU classes have included Martin Luther King, Jr., Medgar Evers,
Rosa Parks, Thurgood Marshall, Ralph Ellison, W. E. B. DuBois . . .
and the list goes on. . . .

Intriguingly enough, struggles within the dominant power structure
and between these black institutions have been almost entirely over matters
of funding or money (or financial problems), politics and the making of
public policies toward higher education. For example, "all the church-
related schools shared in common a desperate need for money, and many
of them led a hand-to-mouth existence" (Quarles 1971, p. 164).

Unfortunately, there was not a lot of money from black alumni or an
established network to raise money at many of these public black state
colleges and universities. And "often, local Black communities helped
these fledgling academies by bringing farm produce to feed students,
working on buildings, and raising money for them" (Jackson, 1996, p.
187). Toward this end, if the institution called *college* "is the most long-
lived and the most distinctive of American schools, with that precarious
stability which characterizes typically American institutions," (Brann
1979, p. 17) what should we call or understand about these black
institutions? Indeed, can we even call them (especially in their formative
development) institutions of higher learning at all? According to Professors
Mary Frances Berry and John W. Blassingame (1982, p. 268), many
black colleges and universities initially did not even deserve their status,
as:

They were engaged primarily in college preparatory work, and the
number of students actually graduating from their college divisions
was small. Yet, many of the schools endured, gradually abolished
their secondary curricular, and early in the twentieth century became
regularly accredited colleges.

Furthermore, are black American models of higher education based
on social injustices, or some kind of racial isolationist philosophy? We
will explore this question later. But we must be cognizant, or it is tacitly

assumed that many black colleges and universities were formed in tandem with white universities because of the enactment of the Morrill Act of 1858. In essence, the Morrill Act provided "a basic incentive" for all federal aid for agricultural and technical training in colleges" (Veysey 1965, p. 159), and "what the states could obtain for nothing, they were likely to take" (Veysey 1965, p. 15). Berry and Blassingame (1982, p. 268) explained it this way:

> Two pieces of legislation also contributed to the development of black institutions of higher learning. The Morrill Acts of 1862 and 1890 established the basis for the development of land-grant colleges. . . . Though the first act had no specific provisions for black education, many southern states took advantage of that legislation by creating or establishing black colleges, such as Alcorn Agricultural and Mechanical Colleges. . . . The result of the second Morrill Act was the growth of a number of black land-grant colleges, including Florida Agriculture and Mechanical and Tennessee Agricultural and Industrial.

The protracted status of blacks within the higher educational system as described in the aforementioned passage is important to understand because there was no way black and white students at that time, especially in the South, could be educated at similar schools. In a time when blacks were considered second-class citizens and less than completely human, the thought of former slaves being educated wasn't taken seriously by the dominate culture – or it was frown upon, and considered outrageous. Nonetheless, "predominately black colleges increased from one in 1854 to more than 100 by the middle of the next century. They were of three general types: church-related colleges, privately endowed colleges, and public colleges" (Franklin and Moss 1994, p. 408).

In this sense, no issue at that time was as troublesome for freed blacks as that of receiving some sort of book learning, or a proper college education. And for many learned and educated blacks, "college shattered forever their acceptance of the white man's characterization of the black as an inferior being"(Berry and Blassingame 1982, p. 269). It is also worth noting that these new black students, eager for knowledge, represented the future source of productivity for the black community. And despite the misgivings and anxieties of whites, black colleges and universities were established anyway. Benjamin Quarles, the late and eminent black historian's account coincides with what has already been said about the earliest establishment of black institutions:

The southern states offered little support to college-level work of Negroes. The Morrill Act of 1862, which provided for the founding and maintenance of Agricultural and mechanical colleges across the nation, was silent about dividing federal funds on a racial basis. Three southern states did, however, made available to Negroes a portion of the funds received from the national treasury (Quarles 1971, p. 164).

It is no wonder that black colleges and universities nationwide had considerable difficulty in their establishment, especially when they were given so much opposition, as in the Deep South. Some attribute this to the awesome power of the Southern White Democrats at that time. In support of this debatable thesis, it is also important to remember that: "The second Morrill Act, passed in 1890, specifically authorized the use of land-grant funds for Negro colleges; it stated that such funds should be "equitably divided" between the white and Negro colleges. But such an equal division was slow in coming. As late as 1916 none of the sixteen existing Negro land-grant institutions was offering college-level work" (Quarles 1971, p. 164).

This important and informative passage by Quarles greatly extends our understanding of how and why black institutions were established in the United States in the first place. Indeed, one of the most remarkable things about black colleges and universities is that they ever existed and survived at all. Nonetheless, "in the closing decades of the century two additional sources of support for Negro schools – state governments in the South and educational foundations established by philanthropists in the North – became available" (Quarles 1971, p. 164).

Additionally, historians have pointed out that although "the Freedmen's Bureau significantly helped only a small percentage of the freedmen [and women], it did leave a lasting legacy, by far its most significant and lasting contribution being in the field of education" (Lindsey 1994, p. 83). This is significant to note because the infamous Freedmen's Bureau provided a critical need and important service to former slaves in that it gave them an avenue of education and learning. More importantly, this newly created and unprecedented government department established "some of the premier universities of today's Black America. . . ." (Jackson 1996, p. 177). In point of fact, "an impressive number of Black colleges and universities . . . , among the most notable being Fisk University, and Howard University," were first assisted by the Freedmen's Bureau (Lindsey 1994, pp. 84-85). According to Professor Howard O. Lindsey, moreover, virtually every aspect of the higher educational system was explored in establishing these institutions. But the most critical or crucial thing, as Lindsey (1994, p. 83) goes on to write was:

> The federally-sponsored Freedmen's Bureau was another institution that tried to care for the needs of all newly-freed slaves. [Furthermore], one of its major duties was to supervise the redistribution of land from Southern plantations to former slaves and poor whites. But the bureau had a difficult time fulfilling its mandate because of its many enemies both in the North and South. A good many Northerners saw the bureau as a waste of time and money, arguing that now that slavery was over, there was no need to give any preferred treatment to the freedmen.

The logic of the above notion on the part of some Northerners (and Southerners), educators, academicians and politicians, however, is utter nonsense, because blacks recently freed from bondage and beginning a precarious and new existence, started out with virtually nothing; nor had they been compensated for their free labor. Therefore, to begrudge them a means of learning in schools was just another way of humiliating, denigrating and denying them what was rightfully theirs: a legitimate education.

Serving, moreover, as the backbone and spiritual aspirations of the black community, "many Black churches [also] founded elementary, high schools and colleges during the Reconstruction" (Lindsey 1994, p. 83). Reconstruction, of course, was that period of reorganization after the Civil War in the South when the Confederate States were forced to give up their complete sovereignty – politically and socially – to become once again a part of the Union or nation. As Berry and Blassingame (1982, pp. 267-268) so aptly noted, "In 1867 the federal government also added to the growing list of higher educational institutions for blacks by establishing Howard University in Washington, D. C. And in 1868, the AMA founded one of the most influential schools in the history of black education, Hampton Institute."

All of this says something of the state of men and women freed from slavery. John Hope Franklin, the distinguished black historian recognized that "While the period of their most rapid growth was the thirty years following the Civil War, the twentieth century witnesses some increase [in these black schools]. States and cities established colleges for education of blacks and also took over church-supported institutions" (Franklin and Moss 1994, p. 408).

Even more important, wealthy white, Jewish philanthropists also played a significant role and part in the early development and establishment of historically black colleges and universities. For example, by helping or assisting black Americans help themselves, Julius Rosenwald, who himself was raised in poverty, "to become president and a major stockholder of Sears, Roebuck and Company," (Stein 1998, p. A22) was to vigorously support black educational institutions (financially) nationwide with his tremendous wealth.

The fact of white philanthropists making substantial contributions to black schools and universities is important to consider because in their own indomitable way, they came to control or influence the direction and course of knowledge and development blacks received, resulting from the entire educational process. And, not surprisingly, "For decades, whites ran these colleges, and the colleges' educational philosophies often reflected their founders' ideas of Black needs in the postwar years. However, Tuskegee, founded by Booker T. Washington, was from the beginning a school staffed entirely by Blacks" (Jackson 1996, p. 186). At that same time, or in these circumstances, "Black intellectuals found it difficult to "make" men and women because whites dominated so many of the black colleges, making up a majority of the faculty, trustees, and presidents. [And] by the early years of the twentieth century, many of these whites had lost the missionary zeal characteristic of their predecessors in the Reconstruction period" (Berry and Blassingame 1982, p. 277).

What is truly lamentable about many black colleges and universities and their black leadership – in the early years and incarnation – is that they were not as influential as white administrators, especially in raising money. Moreover, and even more important, we should not forget, as Berry and Blassingame (1982, p. 275) remind us:

> These early black colleges were originally staffed and administered by [white] teachers from Oberlin, Harvard, and Yale, who tried to make black colleges the counterparts in every detail to the most elite New England colleges. They were sincere in their missionary zeal, and if anything they were often overwhelming in their sense of mission.

It is a complex story that has been repeated time and again in the United States, and as far as black schools of higher education are concerned. In essence, white Americans, provided both moral support and financing (and other aid) to black institutions – for specific reasons –

but later abandoned these lofty goals and left these institutions to fend for themselves. This notion is even more difficult to understand when considering private black colleges, because they were established under different circumstances. Private black colleges, of course, did not have the various state governments or federal agencies to fall back on in terms of providing an infusing of funds when needed and necessary. Indeed, "the genesis of the public-controlled college for Negroes was markedly different from that of the private colleges, and their year-to-year existence was a triumph of frugality and compromise under paternalistic state control" (Gallagher 1971, p. 21). One must also note that the economic and political fortunes of private black universities, as their situations changed over the years, were aggravated "by the decline in support from philanthropic organizations, precipitated in part by the presumption that black colleges were no longer needed, and in part by change in tax laws adversely affecting foundations" (Hughes, *et. al.,* 1995, p. 367).

Conclusions

Everything discussed thus far about African American students, and black colleges and universities has been contentious. But these vitally controversial and important issues, responses, and investigation of the problems, will show that "the continued existence of the [predominantly black] colleges is threatened [today] by falling enrollments, inflated operating costs, and competition with the affluent white institutions for their better-qualified teaching and administrative personnel" (Hughes, *et. al.* 1995, p. 367).

Nevertheless, black students now have more educational opportunities opened up to them, such as having the ability to attend white universities, if desired, and other prominent institutions of higher education. Indeed, "the establishment of black colleges and the acceptance of black students at . . . a number of northern white institutions were the first steps in ending antebellum proscriptions against the acquisition of higher education by Afro-Americans" (Berry and Blassingame 1982, p. 268). Similarly, and according to Franklin and Moss (1994, p. 409), "The significant trends in the higher education of African American became noticeable in the second half of the twentieth century. One was the dramatic increase in the enrollment of blacks in predominantly white colleges and universities. In point of fact, and unquestionably, black institutions have suffered unexpectedly because of the exodus or flight of black students to white universities. Indeed, it became an unfortunate and worrisome fact of life. It is also interesting to recognize or note that "the drain on the 103 historically black institutions of higher education [actually] began with the 1954 Supreme Court decision outlawing school desegregation as college-bound blacks took advantage of opportunities to attend white universities" (Hughes, *et. al.* 1995, p. 367).

Many educators have said that for these reasons, black colleges and universities are increasingly becoming irrelevant, and unnecessary. Nevertheless, and to the contrary, we must be cognizant that "of all Blacks graduating from college, more than 50 percent still received their degrees from black institutions – a reflection of the high attrition rate of black students at white colleges and universities. The statistics tell two stories: one, of the continuing importance of the black colleges; another, of their struggle for survival" (Hughes, *et. al.* 1995, p. 367).

Nothing could demonstrate more clearly the truth of the above statement, but does this mean that by attending a black university will determine whether black students will or not succeed? Moss and Franklin's remarks about the importance of black students at universities are striking. They write:

> By 1977 there were 1.1 million blacks in colleges and universities, accounting for 9.3 percent of the nationwide enrollment. Within a few years, however, there was a noticeable decline in the number of African Americans attending institutions of higher education. By 1984 the number had dropped to 993,574; of these, 267,000 were in historically black institutions, which continued to provide more than half of all the bachelors degrees received by African Americans (Franklin and Moss 1994, p. 409).

The idea, therefore, of dismantling black colleges and universities and incorporating them into the same higher educational school system is a fascinating business, though ultimately not a comforting one, because such black institutions, without a doubt, are places where opportunities abound. As a result, we now have many fine black institutions of higher learning. Franklin and Moss (1994, p. 408) would attest to this fact as they summarize:

> The enrollment of African Americans in institutions of higher learning increased steadily in the years following World War I. By 1933 more than 38,000 blacks were receiving collegiate instruction, and 97 percent

of these students were in colleges in Southern states. Despite the Depression, which forced the curtailment of expenditure, physical plants of black colleges were improved and teachers continued to increase their training.

As one can perhaps surmise, and at every level of the educational process, teaching, researching, and curriculum decisions are made at historically black colleges and universities, just like with predominantly white universities. Hence, black institutions are not only necessary, they are crucial to the educational health and stability of the nation. And although there has been a recent and dramatic decline in the admisssion of blacks at predominantly white schools in the United States, we must acknowledge that "since the early 1970s, in what some see as a deliberate strategy to destroy black institutions, compulsory integration of black colleges has become a heated public policy debate. [Furthermore], proponents argue that the requirement of integration cuts across the board; opponents point out that black schools never had a policy of discriminating against whites" (Hughes, *et. al.* 1995, p. 367).

Why is all this important? It is truly significant because black colleges and universities have never achieved the status of many white institutions in terms of size and prestige, yet they continue to exist, to persist, despite past and future obstacles and problems. In the final analysis, it must be made abundantly clear that:

> The central issue in the maintenance of black colleges is the crucial role they play in preserving black heritage, instilling pride in black youth, and training black leadership. The very fact that such a disproportionate number of black students entering white colleges fail to graduate provides a powerful argument for the psychological and social dimension found at black colleges that is so crucial to achieving academic success (Hughes, *et. al.* 1995, p. 367).

And until we recognize the fact that there is still an urgent need for black colleges and universities, the idea of eliminating them, for supposedly the public good, will continue to persist unabated. The final question then in my mind is: Are we destined forever to have separate higher education programs within the United States? When all is said and done, it remains to be seen, of course, whether these black institutions will continue to exist, even though they have achieved phenomenal results and success in educating the African American student.

References

Bennett, Lerone. 1988. *Before the Mayflower: A History of Black America*. 6th Edition. New York: Penguin Books.

Berry, Mary Frances and Blassingame, John W. 1982. *Long Memory: The Black Experience in America*. New York: Oxford University Press.

Bran, Eva T.H. 1979. *Paradoxes of Education in a Republic*. Chicago: The University of Chicago Press.

Davies, Dick. 1994, March/April. "To Be Educated in the 1990s . . . Nevada Revamps its Core Curriculum." *Silver and Blue Magazine*. Vol. 5. No. 4.

D'Souza, Dinesh. 1991. *Illiberal Education: The Politics of Race and Sex On Campus*. New York: The Free Press.

Fleming, Jacqueline. 1984. *Blacks in College*. San Francisco, California: Jossey-Bass Inc.

Franklin, John Hope and Moss, Alfred A. 1994. *From Slavery to Freedom: A History Of African Americans*. 7th Edition. New York: McGraw-Hill, Inc.

Gallagher, Buell G., editor. 1971. *College and The Black Student: NAACP Tract For The Times*. New York: The Special Contribution Fund of The NAACP.

Gill, Walter. 1991. *Issues in African American Education*. Nashville, Tennessee: Winston-Derek Publishers, Inc.

Hughes, Langston, Milton, Meltzer, Lincoln, C. Eric, and Spencer, John Michael. 1995. *A Pictorial History of African American*, 6th Edition. New York: Crown Publishers, Inc.

Jackson, Kennell. 1996. *America Is Me: 170 Fresh Questions and Answers On Black American History*. New York: Harper Collins Publishers, Inc.

Lindsey, Howard O. 1994. *A History of Black America*. Secaucus, New Jersey: Chartwell Books, Inc.

Manne, Henry G. 1978. "The Political Economy of Modern Universities," in *Education In a Free Society*. Editor, Anne Husted Burleigh. 2nd Printing. Indianapolis, Indiana: Liberty Press.

Parsons, Talcott and Platt, Gerald M. 1973. *The American University*. Cambridge, Massachusetts: Harvard University Press.

Postman, Neil. 1996. *The End of Education: Redefining the Value of School*. New York: Alfred A. Knopf.

Quarles, Benjamin. 1971. *The Negro in the Making of America*. New York: The Macmillan Company.

Reuben, Julie A. 1996. *The Making of The Modern University: Intellectual Transformation and the Marginalization of Morality*. Chicago: The University of Chicago Press.

Sowell, Thomas. 1993. *Inside American Education: The Decline, The Deception, The Dogmas*. New York: The Free Press.

Stringer, Christopher and McKie, Robin. 1996. *African Exodus: The Origins of Modern Humanity*. New York: Henry Holt and Company.

Tonsor, Stephen J. 1978. "Authority, Power, and the University," in *Education in a Free Society*. Editor. Anne Husted Burleigh, Editor. 2nd Printing. Indianapolis, Indiana: Liberty Press.

Veysey, Laurence R. 1965. *The Emergence of the American University*. Chicago: The University of Chicago Press.

Wenglinsky, Harold. 1997. *Students at Historically Black Colleges and Universities: Their Aspirations and Accomplishments*. Princeton, New Jersey: Policy Information Center at the Education Testing Service (ETS).

Wexler, Sanford. 1993. *The Civil Rights Movement: An Eyewitness History*. New York: Facts On File, Inc.

Wickham, DeWayne. 1993, June 21. "Stop Blaming the Victims for Black Separatism." *USA Today*.

Chapter Four

ℰℐℭℛ

Black Studies, and Black Feminism at Colleges and Universities: The Curriculum Debate

Introduction

I am a proponent of tradition when it comes to higher education, steeped in content. Toward this end, I think we must all understand that opinions about education cannot be intelligently found or explored without gathering information on all or many things. Which is to say, we must educate the student in not only the foundations of western civilization, such as reading the classics; but we must also learn to understand other forms of educational exercises, as the process of learning should not be limited to the classroom, or only to one academic source. According to Professor Lawrence W. Levine (1996, p. 160), for instance, "a historical approach means that to understand American culture is not enough to understand only one of its components, no matter how important it may have been."

Professor Levine's astute commentary is important to understand because in a controversy that has stirred deep interest in academic circles in recent years, Black Studies programs at colleges and universities around the country have been attacked, and are once again fighting for their very survival and existence on campus. This is nothing new. It was true even back in 1971, when fledgling Black Studies departments (at many colleges and universities) dropped to 200 from 500 schools that provided full-scale programs (Allen 1974, p. 2). Perhaps the primary reason many such programs, or the Black Studies movement, initially failed was because there was an urgent need to establish them quickly, without careful thought, "planning, or academic enterprises" (Hughes, *et. al.* 1995, p. 368). Therefore, they were not "incorporated as an integral part of the host college or university" (Hughes, *et. al.* 1995, p. 368). Nonetheless, many of these Black Studies programs survived, and continue to exist to this day because they were created with "the same high standards of academic excellence required of other departments" at higher educational institutions (Hughes, *et. al.* 1995, p. 368).

Toward this end, moreover, and with the current racial climate and the end of Affirmative Action at several top-notch colleges and universities, the need for ethnic, feminist and Black Studies programs at both Black and White universities is greater than ever. Investigative journalist S.C. Gwynne (1997, p. 48) writes:

> Anyone curious to know what America's universities might look like in the absence of affirmative action got a chilling glimpse of the future . . . in California and Texas. The best law schools in both states – recently ordered not to consider the race of their applicants – said the number of blacks and Hispanics enrolling . . . had fallen to levels not seen in decades.

What is Black Studies?

The elimination of preferences for Blacks and others at white universities certainly has been a reversal of fortune for minorities in America. Therefore, will this trend continue throughout our nation? Or does this mean that an understanding of Black Studies or the discipline is in further jeopardy? Or will Black Americans have to form more of their own predominantly black colleges and universities? Equally important, will Black Americans be limited as to where they now can go to receive a higher education? Clearly, Black people in the diaspora "have a more urgent need to know what their race has accomplished in America and elsewhere, while whites must recognize what their own race has done to Negroes or Blacks" (Newby 1969, p. 32).

The struggle for educational change, knowledge, and enlightenment does not mean "separate racial and ethnic enclaves on many college campuses" (Sowell 1993, p. 282). Rather, it may and should promote integrated studies in the humanities and social sciences – indeed, broader representation for all in the curriculum, and perhaps even revolutionary changes embodying comparative studies of race and culture (Allen 1974, p.2). More importantly, Black Studies programs can "provide opportunities for black [and white] students to engage one another in serious dialogues of mutual interest, and . . . [Black Studies] programs [can] eventually produce the research and exposition that the search for identity requires" (Hughes, *et. al.* 1995, p. 2).

Black Studies, of course, is perceived as a threat by conservative critics, administrators (or school officials) and educators, because the academic discipline tries to tell the truth about Black history and world events, not to rewrite it or sugar-coat the reality. Indeed, in the recent past, as I. A. Newby (1969, p. 32) has written, "American history [has] too often ignored [Blacks] and reflected the racism which permeates our national life" (Newby 1969, p. 32).

This notion is important to note, because according to conservative columnist and economist Thomas Sowell (1993, p. 71), "Increasing hostility toward Blacks and other racial minorities on college campuses has become so widespread that 'the new racism' has been coined to describe it."

Infusing the Discipline in the Curriculum

Furthermore, we must ask: What measures should (or can) we use to counter the ignorance of ethnocentrism in the classroom? Black Studies supporters would say that the debate of these issues remains fixed in the collective conscious of the higher educational academia. After all, as Kent M. Brudney and John H. Culver (1998, p.1) have pointed out, "The goals of higher education are to provide students with skills and knowledge that will enable them to be successful in their chosen careers, have an understanding of the human experience, appreciate the aesthetic nature of that experience, and have an intellectual foundation conducive to lifelong learning in the years ahead." Indeed, some might ask: How exactly can Black Studies accomplish these objectives?

The answer lies in the need for the student to know about esoteric educational things (or endeavors) besides those taught in their particular

college majors, or fields of concentrations. Indeed, how can *any* student
– black or white – become proficient or completely versed in an area of
study without a holistic approach; or know the absolute truth about the
contributions made by others to world knowledge and history? According
to Professor Alan K. Colon (1984, p. 270):

> Most students enter college with little or no comprehension of the
> Black experience in general and the evolution of contemporary Black
> Studies in particular.   This perplexing phenomenon poses a crucial
> problem, for it retards the progressive development and transmission
> of the Black Studies knowledge base as students need to be minimally
> acquainted with a fundamental history that is not taught in normative
> educational structures and processes.

Conservative scholar Sowell (1993, p. 71), however, argues, "What
is most salient *educationally* . . . is the attempt of multiculturalists [and/
or proponents of Black Studies] to make these beliefs a new orthodoxy,
to be imposed institutionally by the political authorities." This is not
necessarily true, though. What Sowell does not point out, as Allen
(1974, p. 6) reminds us, is: "The university . . . *is* a political institution.
In this way the responsibility for racial tensions on campus is shifted
from the racism of the university and instead blamed on . . . Black
Studies."

Part of the problem is the misperception of what multiculturalism is
supposed to mean. Sowell (1993, p. 71) believes that it is "geared
toward leading students to a set of pre-selected beliefs, rather than toward
developing their own ability to analyze for themselves, or to provide
them with adequate factual knowledge to make their own independent
assessments." Again, this is a falsehood, because Black Studies is just
another way of imparting knowledge about a particular subject.

Other critics, and skeptics, even to this day, wrongly accuse Black
Studies of "having no proper subject matter and of being merely an
attempt to boost the collective black psyche by glorifying black history"
(Allen 1974, p. 6). Accordingly, conservative critics like Dinesh D'
Souza falsely believe that the study of western classics is collapsing beneath
the weight of pressure to provide diversity. This sort of contentious
assertion, of course, is utter nonsense because the curriculums at both
White and Black universities are still predominantly and overwhelmingly
Eurocentric. And these so-called newly introduced disciplines haven't

displaced any predecessor. Where is D' Souza's empirical evidence? He even goes on to write: "Many minority leaders make actual head-counts of the authors and authorities in the curriculum, and they find accusations of white male predominance to be proven right. Why are Plato and Locke and Madison assigned in philosophy class but no black thinkers? How come so few Hispanics are credited with great inventions or discoveries? Feminists ask: "Why is only a small percentage of the literature readings by women" (D' Souza 1991, p. 245)?

These questions are extremely valid, but D' Souza and other conservatives fail to understand that to ask them is the essence of education. To think otherwise, or to deny students a platform or voice on these complex issues, strikes me as pure elitism. Indeed, why shouldn't we gradually infuse in the curriculum various points of view, not confined to one ethnocentric model? The assertions made by Sowell, D' Souza and other opponents of multiculturalism – and Black Studies in particular – are largely untrue. Besides, they all make an old argument. All academic disciplines evolve; if science were taught now as it was half a century ago, the results would be laughable. Those who argue against Black Studies would prefer to freeze the study of literature, history, philosophy, and similar disciplines, where it was half a century ago, when no one questioned that these were white male preserves. Ironically, that would eliminate D' Souza and Sowell from the picture, too. But as historians of the black experience have noted, "The discipline [of Black Studies] was never given the opportunity to mature and was never granted comparable status with other ethnic studies" (Hughes, *et. al.* 1995, p. 368) This, of course, is the point of the matter – and the problem for uniculturalists. Black Studies, finally, encompass two general subjects: "What blacks have done in America, and what whites have done to them. The former encompasses the activities, aspirations, and achievements of the race, the positive side of its history; the latter concerns white racism, the nature and extent of racial discrimination, the patterns of exploration and repression" (Newby 1969, p. 32).

Critics would, of course, disagree with such a radical premise or scholarship, as if students are not smart enough or entitled to possess such knowledge. But do blacks worry or agonize over a belief or philosophy based on something more tangible or relevant than a Eurocentric notion ? Or does Black Studies blend hot button, educational issues that play upon the fears of White America?

Black Feminism and the Problem with the Disciplines

Even more important, and as far as incorporating a black feminist point of view to education and scholarships, I maintain that it is long overdue. Bell Hooks (1994, p. 111), distinguished professor of English at City College in New York, and a radical black feminist writer, would agree that:

> Though the politically progressive clamor is for "diversity," there is little realistic understanding of the ways feminist scholars must change ways of seeing, talking, and thinking if [they] are to speak to the various audiences, the "different" subjects who may be present in one location.

With such a monumental and difficult task of re-thinking, training and teaching Black Studies and Black Feminism, it's a wonder such academic disciplines have taken hold at all in academia. Indeed, as Bell Hooks (1994, p. 112) has commented, "Any curriculum focusing specifically on black women, has been seen as suspect." Such suspicion might lead one to ask: What are we afraid of? Hooks, an insurgent black-intellectual, also writes from a post-modern perspective that denies the old historical notion of blacks as being inferior and the superiority of Eurocentric education. Moreover, many amateurs and full-time, black educational scholars find a great deal of truth and confirmation in what Bell Hooks has to say, no matter how unpleasant or unpopular it is with the rest of the academia.

If Hooks is biased, that is the rule, not the exception. Conservatives may claim a liberal bias in education, but that does nothing to mitigate the salient fact that conservatives have their own prejudices. In fact, if Sowell and D' Souza had read the brilliant Brazilian scholar, Paulo Freire's (1972, p. 64) book, *Pedagogy of the Oppressed*, they would know, "The teacher cannot think for his students, nor can he impose his thought on them. Authentic thinking, thinking that is concerned about *reality*, does not take place in ivory tower isolation, but only in communication." Black Feminism tries to communicate to all students, not just black students. Therefore, Black Studies and Black Feminism are for everyone. Furthermore, the bit of logic previously offered by Freire is exactly what Black Feminism and Black Studies and other such programs are trying to relate or impart: thinking and teaching holistically and realistically. Ultimately, we must also note that Black Feminism and "Black Studies refers to the attempt to create a systematic body of knowledge and of experience based in the history of Black people. [Black Feminism and] Black Studies theory and practice examines and enhances the survival, well-being, development, and perpetuation of people of African origin, particularly those in the United States" (Colon 1984, pp. 268-269).

Criticism of the Disciplines

Contrary to what conservative critics tell us about proponents or supporters of Black Studies and Black Feminism, there is no real coercion or academic forcing of pre-selected beliefs in these important and serious scholarly disciplines. This is a misperception that stems from the essential sense that a Eurocentric world view is superior or universal, and beyond challenging. An educational understanding *is* fundamental, but I am hard pressed to believe that there are any races that are truly superior in general knowledge, ideas, or definite fields of study and scholarship. More importantly, nothing is *sacrosanct* or above question. And that includes challenging orthodox scholarship and knowledge. Bell Hooks (1994, p. 113) writes, "Confronting one another across differences means that we must change ideas about how we learn rather than fearing conflict, we have to find ways to use it as a catalyst for new thinking, for growth. Black students often bring this positive sense of challenge, of rigorous inquiry to feminist studies." Additionally, students bring a sense of wonder to black studies, and the basic canon of scholarship, for the very reason of its freshness.

In fact, Black Feminist Studies should be acknowledged as a way of challenging widely accepted beliefs and practices, to see and understand the world in a different light or as it really is, as well as inspiring debate. Furthermore, why shouldn't we regard the disciplines of Black Studies and Black Feminist Studies as being at the threshold of new and exciting scholarship? Professors Guy Martin and Carlene Young (1984, p. 262) tell us that:

> An investigation of [Black Feminism], African and Afro-American/ Black Studies is instructive and perhaps even prophetic in so far as it represents a microcosmic view of the dialects of power and the never ending struggle of the colonizer and the colonized. The very nature of the introduction of these . . . disciplines into academia provides insight into the character of the society which produced them.

Although the important theories of scholars in ethnic studies are questioned in the academic world, it must be clearly understood that they are not radical disciplines that try to brainwash, indoctrinate, or change the student's conviction about world events and recorded history. More importantly, and in terms of Black Studies are concerned, it is not true that students are unduly influenced by the proponents or teachers in the field. As Freire (1972, p. 64) explains, "If it is true that thought has meaning only when generated by action upon the world, the subordination of students to teachers becomes impossible."

Furthermore, the way blacks – in the past – have been portrayed in scholarly accounts and historical texts have been mostly unflattering and sometimes outright demeaning; therefore, should such prejudicial scholarship, or scientific racism, as exhibited in *The Bell Curve,* be embraced by everyone? Professor Russell L. Adam (1980, pp. 140-141) of Howard University asserts: "The contents of Afro-American studies as a movement and an intellectual concern constitute an *interdisciplinary* enlargement of interest and perception which implicitly and often explicitly go to the roots of values, social structure, and societal dynamics."

What does all this mean? Essentially, black women and black men, in general, have only recently been able to determine how to define their own intellectual place in history and the academia; however, the discipline of Black Studies is not yet in the *pantheon.* Professor Melville J. Herskovits (1948, p. 1) once pointed out that:

> The contribution that the study of New World Negro cultures can make to Africanist research has become apparent only recently, as the data on Afroamerican societies have come to be more adequate, and the concepts and techniques used in studying them have been sharpened.

Russell Adams (1980, p. 140) goes on to suggest that by having a significant number of different students at all universities in the United States, the study of such ethnic or racial groups, and the hiring of appropriate scholars because of diversity becomes important and academically "relevant and useful."

Can it, therefore, be said that Black Studies and Black Feminist Studies are problem-solving or problem-posing disciplines? Indeed, do they give us an appreciation and understanding of our past and educational environments? Again, in the words of Freire (1972, p. 74):

Problem-posing education, as a humanist and liberating praxis, posits as fundamental that men subjected to domination must fight for their emancipation. To that end, it enables teachers and students to become Subjects of the educational process by overcoming authoritarianism and an alienating intellectualism; it also enables men [and women] to overcome their false perception of reality.

Perhaps the biggest concern or controversy universities are having today with Black Studies and Black Feminist Studies programs is: These disciplines try to incorporate a minority pedagogy, or to present a diverse cultural and ethnic point of view. This is the argument. But I suppose the dominant culture will always have a problem with the efforts of such programs.

The Politics of the Attack on Black Studies and Black Feminism

From the start, Black Studies was seen as a subversive enterprise, and those conservatives in the academia loudly proclaimed their displeasure in incorporating the fledgling discipline into the college curriculum. As Professor Houston A. Baker, Jr. (1993, pp. 25-26), from the University of Pennsylvania informs us, "When Blacks Studies came to the university, its detractors immediately cried up an oppositional force of evil and insidious intent – whether this force was imaged as a black ideological contamination of scholarly discourse, a black diminution of standards or a transgressive militancy." Nevertheless, on some college campuses, the conservative efforts were not completely successful, as Black Studies has become a fullfledged academic discipline at many noted universities in the United States.

Similarly, Bell Hooks, the brilliant academician of powerful emotions, also lets us know that the academic community did not [and does not] embrace Black Feminist Studies either. But in recent years, mostly because of Hooks and others, the discipline of Black Feminism has found a niche in the American academy, much to the chagrin of conservative academics. Indeed, one should be cognizant that:

Hooks refutes the antifeminist claim that black women are not victims of sexist oppression nor in need of an autonomous women's movement. She pushes feminist dialogue to new limits [and levels] by claiming that all progressive struggles are significant only when they take place within a broadly defined feminist movement which takes as its starting point that race, class, and sex are immutable facts of human existence (Hooks, 1981).

What Black Studies and Black Feminist Studies do not do, however, is to explain why reputable black scholars, professionals and academics are distancing themselves from amateurs, or *dilettantes* and untrained scholars in the fields. I personally believe that the need for such contact and communication is not only necessary, but it is vital if an understanding of Black Studies, Black Feminism and history is to be accurately recorded. Moreover, it must be understood that *knowledge* in general cannot start in an educational vacuum, or only with one specific paradigm. Many white and black scholars in the field would, perhaps, agree with this bold contention. For example, Dr. Maulana Karenga (1993, p. 11), the creator of *Kwanzaa*, and professor and chair of the Department of Black Studies at California State University, has written:

> Black Studies advocates perceived white studies for the most part as so much propaganda for the established order which not only posed the white paradigm as the most definite of human life and society, but also discouraged study and development of Third World models.

Equally important, a towering figure in the Black Studies Movement, Molefi Kete Asante, has become one of America's best known and respected black scholars, as well as a celebrated and foremost authority of Afrocentricity. For most of his academic career, Asante has rejected the notion that Blacks cannot write cogently and intelligently about their place in American culture at large, and the limitations the dominant culture places on any new way of viewing academic scholarship. Asante also believes that Blacks in the diaspora outside and inside the United States need an Afrocentric, or African-centered perspective for classical Black American scholarship. Asante (1992, pp. 22-23) unabashly reveals his thoughts about the discipline:

> African [Black] American Studies is a discrete discipline with certain critical perspectives, theories, and methods which are necessary for its role in discovery and understanding. Inherent in this statement is the radical idea that African Americans are largely responsible for producing the only new discipline in the social sciences and humanities in the last fifty years.

The contemporary university, with all of its faults, ambiguities, preoccupations and predictability, has often been accused of reneging on the promise to equip the modern-day student with a truly liberal education. However, we must recognize that by providing an understanding of diverse cultures and other new explanations, or opening up the university to diverse educational ideas, we have only enriched and "empowered" the student. As staunch conservative, Levine (1996, p. xviii) has written, "As the university becomes more open to and representative of the diverse peoples, experiences, traditions, and cultures that compose America, its impulse to find explanations for those parts of our history and our culture we have ignored grows proportionately." Levine's explanation and astute reflections are especially true, if certain groups cannot assimilate in America (due to ethnic or racial background), because to ignore the differences of people or minorities within the dominant culture is tantamount to academic genocide or cultural/educational annihilation. In the final analysis, and as professor Ruth Sidel (1994, pp. 99-100) has commented:

> Many academic institutions, concerned about overtly demeaning, sometimes violent behavior as well as the far more subtle denigration of women and other minority groups, have attempted to address these problems through a variety of measures: speech codes; orientation programs for entering students that stress respect for diversity and the importance of civility; curriculum changes that focus on multi-culturalism; hiring policies whose goals are to increase the number of women and members of minority groups on the faculty and staffs of the institution; and the recruitment of more students of color.

What exactly is wrong or truly harmful about fulfilling the above commitments to students and teachers in higher education – or to reach for these lofty or higher educational ideals? Nothing. Ultimately, such measures have enabled "students to comprehend the nature of the society they're part of, the history of groups and traditions they will interact with, [and] the meaning of ideas and experience they will inevitably encounter" (Levine 1996, p. xviii).

Conclusions

In today's volatile and precarious educational climate, and as mentioned elsewhere in this work, it must be understood that for many

Americans, and especially for Black students, the political infighting and the ugly disputes between administrators and educators about whether there is really a need now for Black Studies seem destined for an academic showdown.   Nonetheless, as Robert Allen (1974, p. 2) informed us, "numerous Black Studies departments and programs have not only survived but have established reputations for excellence, and have attracted outstanding faculty and administrators and enthusiastic students." Moreover, according to Brudney and Culver's (1998, p. 1) cogent analyses:

> The key to this enterprise is the idea of "understanding," particularly as it pertains to knowledge.   Students gain knowledge about their specific areas of study through courses in their majors, through knowledge about other topics related to their majors, and through general education courses designed to add breadth to their academic majors.   The end result of this is the "educated person," the university graduate.

Therefore, what purpose should Black Studies and Black Feminism serve in the academy?   Indeed, can other students actually benefit from studying and knowing these disciplines?   Can it be interdisciplinary and totally universal?   More importantly, can the scholarship and research done in the field be a legitimate part of the academic community?   Or will we continue to have problems of integrating and infusing these disciplines in the university curriculum?   Afrocentrist Professor Asa G. Hilliard (1988, p. 42) writes:

> The problems of privilege and oppression in education can be solved. We have sufficient professional knowledge to successfully eradicate both problems from our schools.   That is to say there are no secrets about how to successfully teach students from any racial, cultural, or ethnic group.

Hence, any attempt to introduce and maintain Black Feminism and Black Studies programs at every major university in the United States will continue.   Some additional questions will also be raised, such as: Will Blacks and other minorities be denied a place at the academic table? Or will Blacks also be denied entrance into prestigious colleges and universities because of their race?   Martin and Young (1984, p. 265) have written, "The struggle for Black Studies programs has been an arduous one fraught with many battles, small but sometimes significant successes, and the knowledge that although the struggle is relentless there are no acceptable alternatives." We – or rather – colleges and universities will also be faced with other issues in mastering and outlining these disciplines in the academy. As Colon (1984, p. 269) explains:

> The historical problem confronting Black Studies – the scholarly tradition from which it stems, and, indeed, all alternative movements for African-American educational development – has been that of devising and perpetuating a liberating educational process in a countervailing social cultural/economic climate.

Some final problems and/or thoughts that might be raised that might arouse the ire of some academicians, or create political controversies are: Will the "race card" be played at the higher educational level, giving Blacks an unfair advantage? I personally believe that such opportunities must be made or established for Blacks to redress past discrimination in higher learning and education. More importantly, I believe the "race card" should be played if it is the only way Blacks can level the playing field (at colleges and universities) and win in certain discriminatory and institutional racist situations at the Higher Educational levels. It is difficult, if not impossible, to form any concrete opinions about the future of Black Studies and Black Feminism; however, as professor Terry Kershaw (1989, p. 51) writes:

> As with all new disciplines, its development depends on the continual and critical contributions of its scholars – scholars who are trained in a Black Studies method. Black Studies is ready to take its rightful place in the academy as the leader in the development of research and scholarship focusing on Black experiences.

Unfortunately, there are those in the academia who would have us believe that ethnic experiences are not significant, or there is no need for Black Studies and Black Feminist Studies in American institutions of higher learning. However, one ultimately must be reminded that such academic disciplines are not only significant in the present and future, but, "the failure to recognize [their] importance and to incorporate [them] in America's program of higher education may well prove to be one of the tragedies of the future" (Hughes, *et. al.*, 1995, p. 368).

References

Adams, Russell L. 1980. "Evaluating Professionalism in the Context of Afro-American Studies." *The Western Journal of Black Studies*. Vol. 4. No. 2.

Allen, Robert L. 1974, September. "Politics of the Attack on Black Studies." *The Black Scholar*.

Asante, Molefi. 1992, Summer. "African American Studies: The Future of the Discipline." *The Black Scholar*. Vol. 22. No. 3.

Baker, Houston A. Jr. 1993. *Black Studies, Rap, and the Academy*. Chicago: The University of Chicago Press.

Brudney, Kent M. and Culver, John H. 1998. *Critical Thinking and American Government*. Forth Worth, Texas: Harcourt Brace and Company.

Colon, Alan K. 1984. "Critical Issues in Black Studies: A Selective Analysis." *Journal of Negro Education*. Vol. 53, No. 3.

D'Souza, Dinesh. 1991. *Illiberal Education: The Politics of Race and Sex On Campus*. New York: The Free Press.

Freire, Paulo. 1972. *Pedagogy of the Oppressed*. New York: Herder and Herder.

Gwynne, S. C. 1997, June. "Back to The Future." *Time Magazine*.

Herskovits, Melville J. 1948, January-March. "The Contribution of Afro-American Studies to Africanist Research." *American Anthropologist*. Vol. 50. No. 1.

Hilliard, Asa G. 1988. "Conceptual Confusion and the Persistence of Group Oppression Through Education." *Equality and Excellence: The University of Massachusetts School of Education Quarterly*. Vol. 24. No. 1.

Hooks, Bell. 1994. *Teaching to Transgress: Education as the Practice of Freedom*. New York: Routledge.

Hughes, Langston, Meltzer, Milton, Lincoln, C. Eric and Spencer, Michael Jon. 1995. *A Pictorial History of African Americans*. 6th Revised Edition. New York: Crown Publishers, Inc.

Karenga, Maulana. 1993. *Introduction to Black Studies*. Los Angeles, California: The University of Sankore Press.

Kershaw, Terry. 1989. "The Emerging Paradigm in Black Studies." *The Western Journal of Black Studies*. Vol. 13. No. 1.

Levine, Lawrence W. 1996. *The Opening of the American Mind: Canons, Cultures, and History*. Boston, Massachusetts: Beacon Press.

Martin, Guy and Young, Carlene. 1984. "The Paradox of Separate and Unequal: African Studies and Afro-American Studies." *Journal of Negro Education*. Vol. 53. No. 3.

Newby, I. A. 1969, January. "Historians and Negroes." *The Journal of Negro History*.

Sidel, Ruth. 1994. *Battling Bias: The Struggle for Identity and Community on College Campuses*. New York: Penguin Books.

Sowell, Thomas. 1993. *Inside American Education: The Deadline, The Deception, The Dogmas*. New York: The Free Press.

Chapter Five

ॐ

Molefi Kete Asante and the Legitimacy of Afrocentricity

Evolution of an Idea

Molelfi Kete Asante's book, *Afrocentricity,* is his most provocative and important work, particularly since Afrocentricity has emerged as "a major intellectual concept" (Karenga 1993, p. xiv). *Afrocentricity*, an important work of synthesis, should, therefore, be essential reading to anyone who aspires for a deeper, more personal understanding about the discipline. Asante, an *iconoclastic* scholar in that he tries to attack the settled beliefs and institution of *Eurocentricity* in the United States, has made a name for himself as the nation's foremost authority and "founder of the Afrocentric philosophical movement" (Anderson 1995, p. 116). Asante has also been credited "with coining the term Afrocentricity" (Garland 1995, p. 226).

Although Asante, a revered figure in the Afrocentric movement, is best known for his book, *Afrocentricity* (1988), he has also written *African Culture: The Rhythms of Unity*, co-edited with his wife, Kariamu Welsh Asante, first published by Greenwood Press in 1985; *The Afrocentric Idea*, published in 1990, and *Malcolm X as Cultural Hero and Other Afrocentric Essays*, published in 1993. Asante has also written widely

on speech communication; however, he does not like to be associated
with that part of his academic past. Professor Deborah F. Atwater (1995,
p. 45) explains:

> Because of his visibility in and extraordinary contributions to the field
> of Black Studies, Asante has continued to distance himself from speech
> communication – primarily because he has had to deal with the
> knowledge that speech communication as a field is far too Eurocentric
> and, in many cases, causes African Americans to be in his terms "off-
> center." In short, he found himself at odds with a discipline that did
> not meet his needs.

Asante, a major scholar and celebrity intellectual, as well as a prolific
author continues to awe readers with both the brilliance of his writing on
Afrocentricity and the sheer scope and magnitude of his scholarship.
The books by Asante on Afrocentricity are quintessential, and the work
of an original and deep thinker on the displaced African experience. His
major and seminal book, *The Afrocentric Idea* has reached an enormous
general readership by blacks in the *world* and will undoubtedly continue
to sell, as it is still recommended by many black studies programs
throughout the *diaspora* and United States. It is also used by many
educators of black history.

But like much of Asante's conceptual ideas and writings on
Afrocentrism, some of his works can be hard going, and certainly complex,
but basically his theories are connected, focused and profound. *The
Afrocentric Idea*, especially, is somewhat daunting because of the
interesting and intellectual exercise in African (black) semantics and
definitions; but the work is highly instructive and might be "the starting
point for people seeking a basic explanation of [Afrocentricity]" (Early
1995, p. 36). Critics have even praised Asante's work and writings for
its stylistic, scholarly and daring Afro-cultural notion and interpretive
analysis of world historical events. About *The Afrocentric Idea*, for
example, Henry Louis Gates, Jr., Chairman of the Afro-American Studies
Department at Harvard University has written:

> Asante's wide range of references, his delightful examples taken from
> the black traditions, and his sheer pleasure at discussing black culture,
> all combine to make his argument both cogent and important (Asante
> 1987).

Asante's entire body of work, moreover, provides a theoretical framework for understanding another way of viewing black studies, Afro-American culture and history, especially as black scholars are now prodigiously writing about these matters; and including their bold interpretations of the complicated intellectual genre. Asante's interest in Afrocentrism and Afrocentric writings has galvanized a whole generation of young black people. Indeed, as Asante sees it, the traditional scholar should recognize what has been obvious to him and like-minded scholars or educators from the beginning: Blacks have a history that is separate and distinctly apart from whites, as well as a history that is interconnected or intertwined.

Toward this end, Asante, as well as other important Afrocentrists thinks that there is a way of integrating this Afrocentric-method in the curriculum at all levels of the educational spectrum. Asante does not claim, however, nor has he ever said that Afrocentricity is an exact science, or an absolutely perfect way of imparting knowledge, as in such imprecise disciplines as economics or political science. Which to my mind means, Afrocentrists don't seem to have all of the answers, but at least they are asking the appropriate or right kind of questions about blacks in antiquity, and their future and historical role on this planet, as well as attempting to show and explain the African contribution to world knowledge.

On the other hand, Afrocentricity is not an *anodyne* for all of our problems with teaching diverse cultures or making multicultural education, nor does it relieve our racial tensions, especially in America. It does, however, insist that denying blacks the right to study their established culture (and in their own way) is how the majority protects their elitism or ethnicity and dominance as a factor and way of life. Meanwhile, blacks continue to struggle with their African-American cultural identity. And, in an ultimate affront to the traditional European method of education, black nationalists are demanding an Afrocentrist or African-centered education, which in terms of teaching, is separate and apart from the white cultural mainstream curriculum. But why shouldn't schools diversify to include more than an Eurocentric point of view about African-American culture? Does it mean Afrocentricity will be embraced, but studied less? Asante (1991, p. 46) has stated that: "The task of the Afrocentric curriculum is finding patterns in African-American history and culture that help the teacher place the child in the middle of the intellectual experience." This is not an idea to replace all things European, but to expand the dialogue to include African-American information. As Jerry Adler (1991, p. 42) and others have written:

> Afrocentrism brilliantly exposes how whites have manipulated history and ethnography for their own advantage. In Europe, racist scholars obliterated the influence of whole African civilizations. In antebellum America, science and history were put to work bolstering the case for slavery. But the solution Afrocentrism proposes – in effect, the creation of a separate history for and by black American – is seen by many as a prescription for intellectual apartheid.

But always steering clear of embellishment and the notion of triumphalism in the field, Asante stresses the need to include African-American culture (and heritage) in academic curriculums to preserve and celebrate what little visibility and traditions blacks have – to not be forgotten and become invisible again. Asante (1987, pp. 9-10) has written:

> The Afrocentric analysis reestablishes the centrality of the ancient Kemetic (Egyptian) civilization and the Nile Valley cultural complex as points of reference for an African perspective in much the same way as Greece and Rome serve as reference points for the European world. Thus, the Afrocentrist expands human history by creating a new path for interpretation, making words like *negro* and *colored* obsolete and anachronistic. *African* is identified with time, place, and perspective. Without the Afrocentric perspective the imposition of European line as *universal* hinders cultural understanding and demeans humanity.

As already indicated, Asante has had a long interest in black language (or Black communication), the African continuity of symbols in the Americas, and Afrocentric cultural analyses (Holloway 1990, p. 240). In the course of a splendid academic career, and as the former Chairperson of the Department of African-American Studies at Temple University in Philadelphia, Asante has published 38 books and over 150 professional journal articles. He also edits the *Journal of Black Studies*. About his prolific scholarship and output, Asante has commented: "I am not pleased with my level of production, because I have far more books in my head than I have energy to produce. I think I should at this age probably have produced 55 or 60 books" (Shea 1997, p. A13).

Asante is also credited with transforming the fledgling Afrocentric discipline from a virtually unknown field of study after moving to Temple

University. Afrocentricity is still a relatively new discipline, but most scholars have scant knowledge of the legitimate work done in the field. Indeed, one can perhaps make the claim that many scholars are defiant, or not even warm to (or they perhaps have an unwillingness to know) the whole notion of Afrocentrism. Or maybe this lack of acceptance of the philosophy and theories of Afrocentricity is mere skepticism of the method. About the methodology, Asante (1992, p. 23) has ventured: "The Afrocentric enterprise is framed by cosmological, epistemological, axiological and aesthetic issues. In this regard the Afrocentric method pursues a world voice that is distinctly Africa-centered in relationship to external factors or phenomena. Not . . . distinctly African, which is another issue, but Africa-centered, a theoretical perspective." Professor Terry Kershaw (1992, p. 163) also explains:

> The purpose of generating Afrocentric knowledge is to describe the life experiences: to analyze the effect of forces that impact on life chances: and, to help develop tools designed to change negative forces into positive forces as they impart on the life chances of people of African descent. This pillar connects the Afrocentric scholar with the community because the generating of Afrocentric knowledge begins in the communities of "African" people (Kershaw 1992, p. 163).

Asante and Kershaw's analysis of the Afrocentric method and ideals are extremely important. For some Afrocentricists, the philosophy is a picture of reality for blacks around the world. Afrocentrism then is also a unique movement within the historical perspective (or social context), as it has continuing significance. Afrocentricity, therefore, is a valid discipline because it unabashly responds to the traditionalists' way of excluding blacks of African descent from history. In essence, this tells us that there is another way to look at culture and historical truths besides from a Eurocentric perspective. Asante (1991, p. 46) has written: "Afrocentricity is the belief in centrality of Africans in post modern history. It is our history, our mythology, our creative motif, and our ethos exemplifying our collective will. On basis of our story, we build upon the work of our ancestors who gave signs toward our humanizing function."

Asante is the kind of brilliant academic who believes wholeheartedly in what he writes and teaches; but unfortunately at the same time, he has managed to alienate many white and conservative black scholars in the academic community because he dares to question the traditional method and Eurocentric way of presenting information and knowledge about black people. Among other things, Asante (1991, p. 46) has argued:

> Recent African-American history has shown that we have frequently been imitative of whites, following in the path of Europeans without understanding our own identities. Few African-American students or adults can tell you the names of any of the African ethnic groups that were brought to the Americas during the Great Enslavement; and yet prior to the Civil War there were no African-Americans, merely enslaved Africans. We know European ethnics names, but not these [African] names, because we have seldom participated in our own historical traditions.

Afrocentricity, of course, was conceived and developed with perhaps a conscious need to find meaning and purpose for blacks who have been displaced throughout the world. The focus of Afrocentrism is to teach "history from the African perspective with the beginning of civilization occurring in Africa" (Hill and Hill 1994, p. 10). Afrocentricity is also a result of the *neglect* and *oversight* of white scholars to paint an accurate picture of black culture and the history of blacks in Africa and the African diaspora inside and outside the United States. As pointed out in the *Original African Heritage Study Bible* (1993, p. v), "For too long in the history of Western civilization, persons of African descent have been stereotyped in negative ways which have caused them to question not only their own identity but also their part in God's plan of salvation." Afrocentricity, therefore, looks at history from a totally different perspective, if possible, not confined to ideas in the Eurocentric mode. Asante (1991, p. 46) has written that "Afrocentricity is both theory and practice. In its theoretical aspect it consists of interpretation and analysis from the perspective of African people as subjects rather than as objects on the fringes of the European experience."

Afrocentricity teaches that blacks in the diaspora – or Africans (blacks) that have been dislocated – should take pride in their African history and past, as well as the traditions of heritage and oral culture, even if they never visit or return to the lands of Africa; and that blacks should fight to control how their history is written or recorded. This is important to understand, because "Afrocentrism is often defined broadly as an attempt to purge bias in books and curricula that represent Europe as the cradle of Western culture. The Afrocentric approach emphasizes the experiences, culture, history and traditions of Africans and African-Americans" (Horwitz and Loose 1993, p. A-1).

Ultimately, we must be cognizant that a Eurocentric perspective (or view) is often too narrow to explain the experiences of African-Americans, and other minorities, yet [sic] it "still provides almost all the interpretive tools with which we struggle to understand each other" (Uriate 1997, p. 7B). And this *reality* is the crux of the objection and complaint many blacks have with the traditional Eurocentric method. Which says, the European mode is too rigid and limited to hold all of the answers or explanations we seek to understand our various dilemmas.

On the other hand, radical conservatives like former presidential candidate and political columnist, Pat Buchanan (1997, p. 31) would argue that we need to "strengthen our European core." But would this strengthening be at the expense of excluding blacks and most other minorities in America? Moreover, does Buchanan really believe the oppressive and racist old America (with its dominant European structure) was a good place to live and is "worth preserving" (Buchanan 1997, p. 31)? What exactly was so good about it? And why shouldn't it be loathed? Equally important, why can't the traditional method be questioned? In the final analysis, as Asante (1991, p. 46) tells us, "Afrocentricity is a struggle against extreme misorientation, where many of us believe that we share the same history as whites; indeed, that we came across on the Mayflower." The reality, of course, is: blacks from Africa were brutally subjugated and brought to the Americas in chains, as slaves.

Therefore, is it fair to ask blacks to accept wholeheartedly a one-sided version or account of history as seen and interpreted by whites or Europeans? All in all, what exactly is wrong with "the idea that Africa and persons of African descent must be understood as making significant contributions to world civilizations as proactive subjects within history . . ." (The Original African Study Bible 1993, p. v)? Afrocentricity then is how blacks see their world, with all of the pains, glory, hardships, indifference, apathy, complacency, and problems, without sugar-coating the brutality, rape, pillaging, and destruction of most of the known world done by Europeans. This reality, for example, cannot be forgotten or erased. So Afrocentricity not only recognizes the accomplishments of blacks throughout our historical past, it underscores the importance of presenting *viable* educational options in understanding this rich and complex history.

Moreover, if Asante's pronouncements and outspoken disdain for virtually *everything* supposedly Eurocentric has made him an object of some controversy, he seems to take delight in going against the grain.

Indeed, his very life as a black scholar belies his own traditional or classical training at white, higher educational institutions. But "the very architect of 'Afro-centricity' as a philosophic mode" (Mills 1993, p. 17), Asante has not only stuck his neck out for his beliefs, he has written intelligently and aggressively about Afrocentricity in his defense. I believe that he also welcomes all detractors and thrives on the controversy that surrounds the discipline. But Asante has been touted as – or accused as – being a professor of "blackness" and purveyor of a nonsensical, racial epistemology in the academy.

The Attack on the Discipline of Afrocentricity

Equally important, Afrocentrists have been called *everything* from charlatans to incendiary crackpots. According to journalist Nicholas Leman (1993, p. 43), writing in the *Atlantic Monthly,* Afrocentrism:

> has been attacked so often for being less an academic discipline than a self-esteem enhancement program that its leading figures now routinely insist that it isn't therapeutically motivated and aims only to document the enduring influences of ancient African civilizations.

In some academic quarters, moreover, Afrocentrism is not recognized as a discipline worthy of serious study. And *anyone* who embraces the Afrocentricity label or method is branded a heretic. For example, Asante (1990, p. 38) has written, "The failure of the 'Africanists' to make any real gains against the dominant and dominating white and Western ethos that is at the base of so many of Africa's problems is precisely due to the predicament of contradiction. These Africanists, whether black or as is most often the case, white, are trapped in theoretical and methodological prisons from which they can only escape with great danger to their reputations." But to say that Afrocentricity is not important enough to study is like saying we shouldn't develop *any* new academic disciplines, *ever*. Of course this is ridiculous, because the discussion of Afrocentrism has continued to raise eyebrows in and out of the academic community. Nonetheless, Afrocentricity is often dismissed as scholarly fraud. And for many critics, Asante's work, alone with other Afrocentrists is insignificant – or of no consequence at all. Asante is even shunned by many African American intellectual colleagues who criticize his work. Therefore, as professor Alan K. Colon (1984, p. 274) explains, "in the

America education complex, the study of African-Americans [or Afro-centric complex] as a critical component of the examination of the human experience still is not seen as a valid scholastic enterprise."

Indeed, Afrocentric ideas and theories have drawn quite a bit of criticism from both liberal and conservative academicians. But what is so wrong or fraudulent about saying that "Traditional European-centered teaching of world and American history is culturally biased because it does not reflect the true role of Africa, especially Egypt, in the development of Western civilization" (Cooper 1992, p. A-1)? *Nothing.* Especially when it happens to be true. Dissenters and critics think of Afrocentrism as "pseudo-thinking" and "pseudo-teaching," racial half-truths and *euphemisms*, as does the brilliant Ghanian intellectual, Kwame Anthony Appiah of Harvard University, who writes:

Like most cultural movements at full flood, this Afrocentrism is a composite of truth and error, insight and illusion, moral generosity and meanness. But the most striking thing about it is how thoroughly at home it is in the frameworks of nineteeth-century European thought (Appiah 1993, pp. 24-25).

What exactly does Appiah mean by this bold and provocative statement? It is certainly a confusing thought or point of view. But Appiah (1993, pp. 24-25) goes on:

Once we see the essentially reactive structure of Afrocentrism – that it is simply Eurocentrism turned upside-down – we can understand where its intellectual weaknesses lie. It is not surprising, for example, that in choosing to talk about Egypt and to ignore the rest of Africa and African history, Afrocentrism shares the European prejudice against cultures without writing.

Appiah's analogy is without foundation. Understanding the work of Afrocentrists is not easy, but I wonder if Appiah understands the concepts of Afrocentricity at all. Besides, he is wrong on the points he makes in the above passage, because Afrocentrism is more than just Eurocentrism by another name. For example, and as David Covin (1990, pp. 126-127) has pointed out, "Afrocentricity is a way of life undergirded by a value system and a religious orientation. . . .[It] includes every element of human orientation or culture; perception, religion, science, history, philosophy, aesthetics, communication, interpersonal relationships,

psychology, architecture, politics, language, economics, and fashion."
In other words, Afrocentricity covers the whole *spectrum* of black history,
or a whole-world approach to black studies – not just the focusing on
Egypt; although Egypt is very important to Afrocentrists in terms of a
historical reference point. Professor Gerald Early (1995, p. 36) has
accurately assessed that: "We know from scientific evidence that Africa
is the place of origin for human life. If it is also true that Egypt is the
oldest civilization from which Europeans borrowed freely, then Africans
helped shape Western culture and were major actors in history, not bit
players in the unfolding drama of European dominance." Nevertheless,
the claim that Egypt is the cradle of Western civilization has upset many
in the academia. Moreover, as Asante (1991, p. 46) has explained,
"Afrocentricity is not racist nor Anti-Semitic; it is about placing African
people within our own historical framework. In none of the major works
of Afrocentricity has there ever been a hint of racism, ethnocentrism or
anti anybody." In this vein, Asante is as precise in his understanding of
Afro-centricity as he is in his prose. Indeed, he unostentatiously outlines
an impressive amount of knowledge on every aspect of the subject. There
are those, however, who would disagree. For example, journalist
Lawrence Auster (1991, p. 30) believes that an influx of "multiculturalism" and other disciplines and ideas like Afrocentricity on college
and university campuses "creates a dangerous impetus toward ethnic
chauvinism" (Rogers 1994, p. 8).

Conservative intellectuals and dissenters also argue that Afrocentrism
threatens a color-blind society and a Eurocentric America that is
supposedly crucial for a nationalistic state. Professor Diane Ravitch, for
example, has stated, "The pluralists say, in effect, 'American culture'
belongs to us, all of us; the United States is us, and we remake it in every
generation. . . . Ethnocentrism is not multicultural education. It's the
opposite" (Asante 1990, p. 11). But it must be clearly understood that
Afrocentrism is not necessarily part of the multicultural mandate. Which
is to say, Afrocentrism is a separate discipline in and of itself. More
importantly, we have *never* had a color-blind society, nor will we ever
have one (at least in the near future). Equally important, we must ask
the question: Will we ever bridge the 'racial divide' in America? Even
the eminent neoconservative scholar, Nathan Glazer has recently conceded
that we need "a de-emphasis of European culture and greater stress on
ethnic subgroups than on a general American identity" (Shea 1997, p.
A18). And Afrocentricity nicely accommodates or fills this void.

Professor Asante, moreover, remains impervious to the controversy that surrounds the Afrocentric concept. He is not, however, entirely indifferent to criticism. And although his critics and detractors deride him as being a "pseudo-scholar" on Africa, and myth-maker of confusing facts with fiction, especially about Egypt and Greece, it cannot be said that he is self-indulgent, or lazy in his innovative scholarship, for he is thorough and reflective in using the various ancient and contemporary research sources to advance his theories about Afrocentrism. Nonetheless, writes Henty Louis Gates, "Afrocentrists downgrade the significance of Western culture yet go to much trouble to claim authorship of it" (Adler 1991, p. 42).

Furthermore, the Afrocentric philosophy has caused some consternation, criticism, and speculation among journalists – and especially with Egyptian and Greek scholars – in recent years. Afrocentrists have also drawn a wave of denunciation from right-wing groups and rejectionists who find African thought or black or Afrocentric thought offensive. For example, Jim Sleeper (1997, p. 110), the veteran newspaper columnist, has observed:

> Afrocentrists who object that the West owes many of its own conceptual and even technological powers to ancient African civilizations like Egypt never explain why those purported advances didn't penetrate Sub-Saharan Africa beyond Nubia and Kush.

But one must ask in turn: Why is this important? And what Afrocentrists object to the West for not giving credit to ancient Egypt for its civilization and cultural achievements? Unfortunately, Sleeper never tells us about these un-named Afrocentrists.

The traditionalists' persistent and relentless criticism of Afrocentricity – that is, implicitly of their methodology — is nothing new. Research Fellow at the American Enterprise Institute, Dinesh D'Souza (1995, p. 381), demonstrated this contention in his book, *The End of Racism*, when he wrote:

> Afrocentrism is . . . both pathetic and formidable: pathetic because it offers young blacks nothing in the way knowledge and skills that are required by the modern environment; formidable, because it offers them racial dynamite instead: a fortified chauvinism, a hardened conspiratorial mindset, and a robotic dedication to ideologies of blackness.

If what D'Souza says is true, why has the Afro-centered doctoral program at Temple University (to name just one program now in the United States) "produced 42 Ph.D.'s [where] at least 26 [graduates] have found jobs in academe . . . [and] "four are the heads of programs or research centers in the field" (Magner 1997, p. A13)? Ostensibly, D'Souza's quasi-scholarly approach combines disjointed pieces of work from various sources about Afrocentricity to provoke a response to gain attention for himself (Fields 1995, p. 3A). Perhaps D'Souza considers himself a latter-day Gunnar Mydral, who wrote the famous *An American Dilemma: The Negro Problem and Modern Democracy* of 1944, where he eloquently discussed race relations in the United States. But D'Souza is no Mydral.

A healthy skepticism is necessary, but an all-out attack on Afrocentrism, as asserted by D'Souza and others in most of his work on the black experience in America, is quite unnecessary, especially if you have no scholarly credentials (like D'Souza) or empirical data in which to base your comments. Although the African-American community is far more diverse than we would like to believe, Afrocentrism becomes the starting point or point of departure when addressing such complex issues. But if it was up to D'Souza, a provocateur and man-of-color, originally from India, the traditional European approach to scholarship is quite acceptable, and never should be questioned, even if such a mode continues to dehumanize blacks, and other minorities.

In truth, D'Souza's ideas do not add much in the way of the subject. Which might lead one to ask: Who even invited him to the academic discussion? Indeed, D'Souza's interpretation and writings about Afrocentrism become uncharacteristically contrived and strained with such matters as who were the Egyptians and whether certain Greeks were blacks. Henry Louis Gates writes: "what would it prove even if Plato himself were black" (Adler 1991, p. 45)? For the record, as Asante (1996, p. 32) tells us: "Afrocentrists do not spend time arguing that either Socrates or Cleopatra were Black. I have never seen these ideas written by an Afrocentrist, nor have I heard them discussed in any Afrocentric intellectual forums." In other words, the notion of whether Egyptians were black is irrelevant.

D'Souza puts forward pathetic and disjointed generalizations – especially about what he thinks about Afrocentricity – that has been challenged by recent and more enlightened scholarship, by even white academics. For example, Cornell University professor Martin Bernal "argues that racism has pervaded our interpretation of ancient cultures and that Egypt contributed greatly to the Greek civilization that many, especially Americans of European ancestry, view as the foundation of Western culture" (Specter 1990, p. A-3). Toward this end, Asante (1996, p. 32) has long espoused the view that "you cannot begin the discussion of world history with the Greeks." As one can perhaps ascertain, Asante has always had a strong feeling for what is central and important to Afrocentrists. He certainly has the intellectual and emotional energy to sustain the Afrocentric movement. More importantly, Asante has never taken a cavalier approach to the subject.

Among some black intellectuals and skeptics, however, like Cornel West, who believes in "Marxist pragmatics and Christian hopes," and especially "Black points of references for studying historical situations, *but not* Afrocentricity" (Hooks and West 1991, p. 5), Asante has had this to say:

> We [Afrocentrists] claim that there is nothing more correct for African-American people than our own experiences, if we learn from them. . . . Our solutions are within ourselves, not outside of us. . . . West finds his intellectual center in white tradition. He [West] has been educated away from himself" (Mills 1993, pp. 17-18).

What West perhaps doesn't realize is – all blacks have a story to tell, exaggerated or not. I think West knows this. Indeed, are we not enriched, for example, from the early slave narratives that are not always precise or historically accurate? Ultimately, Afrocentrists should not become apologists for their thoughts and philosophy. In recent years there has also been a number of distortions, mis-statements and misperceptions about what *exactly* is Afrocentrism. These falsehoods and distortions hide any and all alternative ethos and ways of understanding the major issues of the Afrocentric method.

Indeed, in a controversy over Afrocentrism that has stirred deep interest in academic circles, Professor Mary Lefkowitz of Wellesley College leveled an attack at Asante and other Afrocentrists in her book, *Not Out of Africa*. Lefkowitz, trained as a Greek classicist, has written widely and extensively about so-called Afrocentric myth of ancient history. She has also condemned Afrocentrism as being insufficiently serious for academic discussion, and labeled Asante as excessive. At the same time, Lefkowitz says that Afrocentrists play loose with the facts repeatedly, that they lack rigor, discipline and careful reflection of the material.

This is not surprising, given her lack of Egyptian or African knowledge. And as Asante (1996, pp. 68-69) cogently explains:

> *Not Out of Africa* has demonstrated the tremendous power of a false idea, especially when it is advanced in the halls of the academy. I have come to believe that it is a part of a larger falsification that encompasses the various right-wing ideologies that parade as truth. They are rooted in the same dogma: Reason is the gift of the Greeks. The Greeks are Europeans. Europeans are White. White people gave the world reason and philosophy. This not only is a bad idea, it is a false idea. It is a bad idea because it preaches a European truimphalism, and it is a false idea because the history record is contrary.

Professor Lefkowitz's main point by contrast, however, is to demonstrate the falseness of Afro-centric history and Asante's notion that: "Afrocentrism is not simply an alternative interpretation of history, offered on the basis of complex data or ambiguities in the evidence: there is simply no reason to deprive the Greeks of the credit for their own achievements"(Lefkowits 1996, p. 7). But exactly who said the Greeks should be deprived of anything? Certainly not the Afrocentrists.

Indeed, according to Lefkowitz, this way of looking at things is simply not true (she emphatically argues), presenting her book as a kind of inverse of the Afrocentrists' claims. The point of her book, after all, is to dismantle the whole idea of African-American thought on the origins of Western civilization. In concentrating on the Afrocentrist argument of the "Out of Africa Theory," she inevitably fails to do justice to the Afrocentrists' entire body of work in this field, which gives us an astonishingly unique and different way of investigating and interpreting African and African-American culture. Perhaps because it goes against the traditional European centered teaching methods in higher education, "where it jostles the established paradigms in ancient history" (Sundiata 1996, p. B3).

But to casually deny others a *platform* to give their thoughts, opinions, and ideas is counterproductive and goes against academic freedom, especially when that learning is vague or ambiguous in the first place. Lefkowitz's brusque refusal to acknowledge that there could be another method of interpreting Greek and Egyptian history and philosophy is sheer elitism. *Not Out of Africa* is also aesthetically offensive, because Lefkowitz's cursory treatment of the subject lets us know that she is *unwilling* to understand all of the intricacies of Afro-centrism. Moreover, her repetitive style is boring and too judgmental. She teaches or tells us nothing about the positive aspects or *intrinsic* values of Afrocentrism, or she presents nothing about where the strengths might lie with the discipline. It is more a weak intellectual and futile exercise that goes over old ground, without pointing out *anything* new about the subject. For example, Lefkowitz (1992, p. 32) writes:

> It is axiomatic for the Afrocentric authors that there has been, since antiquity, a European conspiracy to suppress evidence of African origins, and therefore any argument that a European makes against them, especially on the basis of European writings, ancient or modern, can be regarded ipso facto as invalid.

From the above passage we can see that Lefkowitz is not interested in *understanding* the basic principles or tenets of Afrocentrism, because she is wrong about what the discipline is really trying to achieve. She patronizingly assumes that she knows more about the subject than reputable black scholars (like Asante) have been writing about and studying for years. Asante's sources and rigorous scholarship are certainly more insightful and plentiful than Lefkowitz's written diatribe about the various problems with Afrocentricity; and I believe he deserves a more balance critique.

Lefkowitz also believes that glorifying an Afrocentric method and teaching such courses are tantamount to intellectual and academic heresy. She cannot be tolerant of such courses of Afrocentricity at the university level or *any* educational level, because she is offended by other approaches that view history differently. As Asante (1996, pp. 68-69) has pointed out, "Tragically, the idea that Europeans have some different intellectual or scientific ability is an accepted doctrine, and some scholars will go to any length to try to uphold it."

It is inevitable, Lefkowitz (1996, p. 7) bemoans, that "Afrocentrists are demanding that ordinary historical methodology be discarded in favor of a system of their own choosing. This system allows them to ignore chronology and facts if they are inconvenient for their purposes. In other words, their historical methodology allows them to alter the course of history to meet their own specific needs."

It goes without saying that her tedious wordplay and disguised attacks are not well thought-out, nor are they definitive or pathbreaking. We have all heard Lefkowitz's arguments before, and they are mostly false or untrue. Although conservative columnist, George F. Will (1996, p. 78), would disagree, as he believes "Afrocentrism is an attempt to "empower" African-Americans with "transforming myth." About Lefkowitz, Will (1996, p. 78) tells us that [she] "brings her formidable erudition to bear on the Afrocentrists assertions . . . with heroic patience and goodwill."

But I believe there is *nothing* heroic about Lefkowitz's book, *Not Out of Africa*. And Afrocentrists must not be patronized by her supposed patience, as if she is the great "white mother" overwatching and correcting her little misguided children. Nevertheless, Lefkowitz's book may rival moderate Arthur Schlesinger's *Disuniting of America* and his thinly veiled attack on Afrocentrism, because she too denounces the works of Afrocentrists without really knowing their true philosophy. Lefkowitz believes she has an idea, however. George Will, moreover, is just as *negative* about Afrocentrism, as he considers the writings of Afrocentrists as hodgepodges of pseudo-scholarly work. Will (1996, p. 78) would also have us believe:

> Afrocentrism is another weed fertilized by the idea that there is no such thing as truth, only competing "narratives"; that power decides which narratives prevail; and that people of color are oppressed because the Eurocentric narrative has been "privileged" by the "hegemony" of white racism. Afrocentrists begin with, because Afrocentrism depends on, disdain for historical methodology.

Will, of course, is wrong about this point. And what he and Lefkowitz and other dissenters also fail to realize is that part of *myth* (which they claim the Afrocentrists teach), is rooted in reality. Therefore, why can't we have new philosophic ways and methodologies (that Afrocentrists often use) which will allow us to have an appreciation of African-American history and culture – or a means to explain black history, or changing historical circumstances? Will (1996, p. 78) further writes:

> Afrocentrism is sometimes based on merely incompetent interpretations of facts, but more often is based on aggressively meretricious misrepresentations of facts for ideological purposes. They are the purposes of identity politics, which preaches that in arguments about history, the important thing is not the historians' motives, which are explained by racial or ethnic determinism.

With such callous misstatements made by Will and other detractors, one can easily conclude that they will continue to unnecessarily impede the discipline of Afrocentricity by their condescending and considerable negativity. Clearly, as Professor Abu Shardow Abarry (1990, pp. 123-144) has pointed out, "Afrocentrists have argued cogently that the acceptance and due recognition of all perspectives is far more likely to lead to genuine human knowledge and inter-cultural understanding than reliance on one absolute [European] worldview."

Lefkowitz, however, would perhaps disagree with Abarry, but she too uses a number of secondary sources for *Not Out of Africa*. It must also be noted that she never once visited Egypt to explore Afroasiatic points of view prior to writing her insights and book, as she likewised visited Greece for her scholarly writings in the classics. Lefkowitz (1996, p. 161) even admitted that "As a classicist," [she] "may overemphasize the achievements of the Greeks because [she does] not know enough about the rest of the Mediterranean world. . . ." If what Lefkowitz writes is true, why would she think she is qualified to criticize or write about Afrocentrism? Yes, Lefkowitz examined the scattered documents that are available to write her scathing and bitter book, but she failed to even look at – or acknowledge – all of Asante's works on the subject. I firmly believe this was a mistake on her part.

Lefkowitz even has the temerity to attack Martin Bernal's scholarly inquiry, *Black Athena*, which offers historiographical proof of the Egyptian origins of Greek knowledge. At the height of controversy, Bernal, a white scholar of Government Studies at Cornell University, in the traditionalist sense, presents a masterful work of impeccable research on the notion of African scholarship. Bernal's thesis is that the Greeks did indeed acquire their knowledge and traditions of classical civilization from ancient Egypt, but this fact has always been ignored in history for racist reasons (Bernal 1987).

Lefkowitz, of course, tells us that, as an academic interloper, Bernal's work lacks any definitive information in the field. That is to say, from proclaiming his grandiose conclusions about the *connection* between Egypt and Greece, to his claim of Africa being the cradle of Western civilization (as incontrovertible fact). And curiously enough, Lefkowitz even hints that Bernal draws upon circumstantial evidence rather than *irrefutable* scholarly research. In another instance, Lefkowitz (1996, p. 34) wrote:

> Bernal relies too much on Herodotus's treatment of Egypt. . . . [She goes on] Bernal cites Herodotus on the Egyptian origin of Greek religion and ritual, discussing the many rough but intriguing parallels that can be drawn between Egyptian and Greek myth and cult. Nor does Bernal show how the Greeks came to borrow their "Philosophy" as well.

But can we believe Lefkowitz's speculative scholarship and superficial analysis of the African model over Bernal's definitive *Black Athena*, where he provides us with a wealth of details about the subject, as well as recent, and timely and historical findings about Africa? Lefkowitz (1996, p. 34) even admitted that Bernal's extensively documented work "is more sophisticated, his etymologies more systematic and scientific."

The problem with Lefkowitz's scathing analysis is it is just too *didactic*: she gives us all what she believes is wrong with Afrocentrism or the Bernal Model, with sweeping statements of criticism; but in the final analysis, she doesn't really lend *any* special insight to the African aesthetic. The fact that *Not Out of Africa* was written by an unskilled Egyptian scholar, without much knowledge even in the area, should also tell us something about her motives.

Ultimately, it is the dissenters and detractors who bring up the so-called myths of Afrocentricity, but the literature from legitimate and reputable practitioners in the field does not support such irrationality. Indeed, this is the central fallacy of the Afrocentric-dissenters who believe Afrocentrism is pseudo-scholarship. To the contrary, and in the view and philosophical outlook of many Afrocentrists, the discipline of Afrocentricity offers "a valid procedure through which genuine and healthy scholarship on African peoples can be pursued without the trappings of Europe masquerading as the universal and absolute" (Abarry 1990, p. 123).

Demystifying Afrocentricity or Africology

The demand by black students for such scholarship and interested independent scholars to be "empowered" by what they have learned about African-centered knowledge is becoming increasingly important. Perhaps this can be seen as the widespread dissatisfaction of blacks in getting their historical record and stories explained by white scholars. Equally important, and as Henry Louis Gates (1991, p. 47) has accurately pointed out, "The truth is, too many people still regard African-American studies primarily as a way to rediscover a lost cultural identity – or invent one that never quite existed. And while we can understand these impulses, those in our field must remember that we are scholars first, not polemicists."

The attack on Afrocentrism is hardly unique and different from what has been written already about other unorthodox ideas, scholarship and educational disciplines during their early or formative years. But we must remember that history is developed from premises and situations that, no matter how fanciful, are logical extensions of *wholeness* – politically, socially, as well as economically. Therefore, there must be room for critical analysis. In essence, Afrocentrism must be completely scrutinized just like all other academic disciplines.

Although Afrocentricity may sound objectionable, and even counter productive toward a pluralistic nation, as Schlesinger contends, the method can work hand-in-hand, and along side of the dominant power or culture. But it must be treated inarguably as an alternative way of gaining knowledge of a different kind – and not altogether dismissed. Which is to say, the writings and philosophy of Afrocentrism, like it or not, are inextricably intertwined with America's intellectual community. But to respond to the work in the education field fairly, with integrity and an open mind is a momentous thing to ask, especially when the concept is being attacked before it is completely understood or accepted. Moreover, we still need to explore the possibilities of the discipline to determine the merit and validity of the courses taught in any given class or curriculum.

Furthermore, Afrocentrists must not invent, fabricate, or make things up about Africa or African American history. Scholars can be imaginative in their way of interpreting and presenting history and various works and ancient materials of others – bringing together or folding in all perspectives, ideas and concepts and factual points of view – into a cohesive whole, but it must not be about myths or falsehoods. Legends, on the other hand, are a different story because all legends have a basis in fact. Nor must there be pretension in the field of Afrocentrism.

Falsehoods and myths must never be taught as history, nor must ideas about such matters be taught as history, nor must ideas about such matters be taught in our American colleges and universities as historical facts. However, myths and legends can be looked upon as viable pedagogical tools, or novel ways of teaching and understanding tradition. In other words, myths can be taught, but scholars must explain these notions in the right intellectual, educational or cultural context.

"Doctoring" facts from history can also be detrimental to the Afrocentric cause, as it *devalues* and lessens one's ability to distinguish between reality and fiction. Therefore, Afrocentrists must be extremely accurate and rigorous when it comes to disseminating information and data from a non-white or European point of view. How should this be accomplished? One must be assured that Afrocentrists have done their homework, as well as extensive research, because by not doing so will only add ammunition and fuel to the fire for conservative and liberal detractors.

Moreover, in order to insure there are no errors in the discipline, Afrocentrists must visit the areas of the particular African nation in which he or she writes – carefully studying documents and the language – to be sure they know their works are reflected and discussed properly. In short, Afrocentrists must write and speak the truth, without false embellishment. Additionally, we must also understand that "while serious full-time scholars of the black past are, step by step, still trying to sort out historic fact from fiction, Afrocentrists *dilettantes* [continue to make] dogmatic assertions of black cultural and inventive priority" (Adams 1993, p. A-21). Unfortunately, this unnecessary posturing actually hurts the discipline.

Nonetheless, the Afrocentric mythology is not the point. Historical *accuracy* from a Afrocentric point of view is. Many black or African-Americans have long felt disenfranchised or disheartened by white scholars and their sometimes one-sided writings of African history. After all, we must know that "the greatest benefit of Afrocentricity is a humanistic one. It places the culture of people of African ancestry on an equal plane with all other cultures" (Monges 1997, p. B-10).

Peoples of the African diaspora and or throughout the planet must be told that they too have been a part of world history, that they have made contributions to not only Egyptian, Greek and other African and foreign civilizations, but they also contributed to Western civilizations; particularly the part they have played in creating and establishing the new world or the modern day Americas. Asante (1990, p. 38) writes "Trained in Eurocentric perspectives most contemporary scholars have only seen from a Eurocentric view point and this view is decidedly different from that of the African person who has been victimized by the imposition of Eurocentric expression. Afrocentricity is inevitably the philosophy of African scholarship in this historical movement." Asante's rhetoric is a reminder that much of the world do not see blacks as exploited, oppressed, or as we see ourselves. But as Henry Louis Gates (1991, p. 47) has written, Afrocentricity or "African-American studies is not just for blacks; our subjects is open to all – to study or to teach. The fundamental premise of the academy is that all things ultimately are knowable; all are therefore teachable."

Afrocentrism is an attempt to educate individuals with basic infor-mation regarding black people. Where other black scholars temporize, adulterate and write untruths about black history, Asante tries to tell the truth about African culture, the black aesthetic discourse, and African heritage. And as Russell L. Adams (1993, p. A-21) has explained:

> The African American scholarly community is only now reaching a level where a substantial number of its members can even begin to try to independently validate some of the claims of the passionate amateurs upon whom the press lavishes so much attention.

In terms of influence, Asante has had a profound effect on the minds of a whole group of young black intellectuals and scholars, as he provides insight into the continuing struggle of Afrocentrists to legitimize. Indeed, when you think of Asante's tremendous influence, it has been mostly positive, especially to young black students and serious scholars. He has also transcended the Eurocentric notion of learning and teaching. But Afrocentrism is a field of study that is still seeking respectability. Writes Professor Early (1995, p. 39): "Afrocentrism has succeeded not only in intellectual spheres but on the grass-roots level as well. Its triumph as the legitimation of the black mind and the black aesthetic vision. . . ."

Afrocentricity succeeds also because Asante has taken great pains to explain why nay-sayers and conservative critics have wrongly attacked the ideas and principles of Afrocentrism. To those who know him, and have worked as graduate students under his tutelage, Asante is still a respected professor at Temple University, "who established the country's first Ph. D. program in black studies in 1988," and "built an international reputation for himself, and [the] department as a home for Afrocentrism" (Magner 1997, p. A-13).

Asante, considered an icon in the Afrocentric and black studies community, is now in the most advantageous position of his academic career thus far. Now he has the time "to concentrate [more] on his writing and speaking engagements" (Magner 1997, p. A-13). Indeed, Asante's writings, lectures and teaching, along with the works of Maulana Ron Karenga, Asa G. Hilliard and other legitimate Afrocentrists in the field are an important force in the study of black culture, and must be read, because as Asante has stated, "if you're going to write on Afrocentrism, you can't avoid my work. Like if you're going to write about existentialism, you ought to know something about Heidegger and Sartre" (Magner 1997, p. A-14).

Many of Asante's critics and dissenters, however, judge him on ideas of legitimacy, not the content of his work and the fact that he has shed important new light on the African-centered intellectual scholarship milieu. For example, when Asante writes about African theory, he proves to be an eloquent spokesman for the movement, aware that scrupulous care and attention must be given to the method of analysis in the discipline. Asante (1990, pp. 38-39) has written, "the Afrocentric method approaches all African phenomena from the standpoint of African centrality. Naturally this centrality cannot be left to chance, it must respond to a theoretical framework where each phenomenon is examined within the context of the authentic empiricism so fundamental to the methodology."

Asante's deeper purpose is to scrutinize and use what has been written and already analyzed by all scholarly disciplines. In doing so, Afrocentrists need not denote a compromise with educational standards, and quality. Asante, of course, is also credited with adding intellectual rigor and academic discipline to Afrocentrism. That Afrocentrism, nonetheless, stirs up frustration and controversy in the academia still is irrefutable, and expected.

The thing most conspicuously missing, however, from the many detractors' argument is: blacks cannot assimilate in this society because of the color of their skin, and perhaps Afrocentricity "is the price America is paying for its inability or unwillingness to incorporate into its society African-Americans, in the same way and to the same degree it has incorporated so many [other] groups" (Shea 1997, p. A-16). Christopher Shea (1997, p. A-16) has rightly argued:

> While Asian Americans and Hispanics have followed much the same pattern as the Jews and Italians who came before them, blacks simply have not. They have had too many obstacles placed in their path, for too long. . . . [African Americans] want to live in integrated neighborhoods, surveys show, but whites flee when they do. They want integrated schools, but they run into white flight there, too.

If Shea is correct, and especially if black people cannot or will not assimilate into mainstream American culture, shouldn't they create their own ways of describing and studying this *African phenomenon* or their African heritage? More importantly, should there be an infusion of Afrocentrism into the curriculums at all American Universities? Or is Afrocentrism an exercise in futility? Hopefully, Asante's large body of idiosyncratic and important work will not go unnoticed.

In recent years, Asante has advanced the notion of *Africology*, which is another way of considering or looking at Afrocentricity. Asante (1996,

p. 27) defines Africology "as the Afro-centric study of phenomena, events, ideas, and personalities related to Africa. The mere study of African phenomena is not Africology, but some other intellectual enterprises." This is significant because academics finally will have the opportunity to study a discipline at the threshold of its future development. However, it will take Asante and others to solve a daunting problem: Can Afrocentricity become a respected scholarly discipline? Or will it eventually fade from the academic scene? According to Early (1995, p. 39), "Afrocentrism may eventually wane in the black community but probably not very soon. Moreover, a certain type of nationalistic mood, a kind of racial preoccupation, will always exist among blacks." Therefore, it is a social phenomenon that will not go away or fade easily.

Asante addresses the difficult issue and meaning of Afrocentrism. He has also been trying to demystify Afrocentric thought. Which is to say, Asante provides a succinct and engrossing way of bringing the history and culture of blacks into focus and at the forefront of American education. Asante tells us that:

> Afrocentricity repudiates the imprisonment of knowledge while not repudiating the right of Europe to view the world from its cultural center. It must not, however, be permitted to impose that view as universal. The evaluation of the Afrocentric enterprise must be carried out in congruence with the demands of the discipline in relationship to the centrality of the African historical experience (Kershaw 1992, pp. 163-164).

Asante's works are authentic, as well as interesting, and aimed largely at understanding black people in the diaspora and Africa. In the final analysis, Afrocentricity means "the knowledge base must come from the life experiences of people of African descent; the specific purpose of knowledge generated is to empower Black people to effect positive social change and to describe Black life experiences as determined by Black people's understandings, interests and experiences . . ." (Sailer 1997, p. 52).

When all is said and done, I believe Afrocentrism is worthy of special and scholarly examination, now and in the immediate future. Hopefully, a cultural and historical awareness of blacks in America and elsewhere will make all of us proud. The question that remains is: Can Afrocentrism legitimately take its rightful place among the many other educational and scholarly disciplines, or is it "making itself increasingly irrelevant to the central problems of out society" (Sailer 1997, p. 52)?

References

Abarry, Shardow Abu. 1990, December 2. "Afrocentricity Introduction." *Journal of Black Studies*, Vol. 21.

Adams, Russell L. 1993, September 9. "Neophytes in Afrocentrism." *The Washington Post*.

Adler, Jerry, Manly, Howard, Smith Nern E., Chideya, Farai, and Wilson, Larry. 1991, September. "African Dreams." *Newsweek*.

Anderson, Tony. 1995. "Blowing Smoke: Exposing Empty Criticism of Afrocentricity." *Molefi Kete Asante and Afrocentricity: In Praise and Criticism*. Dhyana Ziegler, Editor. Nashville, Tennessee: James C. Winston Publishing Company.

Appiah, Anthony Kwame. 1993, February. "Europe Upside Down: Fallacies of the New Afrocentrism." *The Times Literary Supplement*.

Appiah, Anthony Kwame. 1997, October 9. "The Multiculturalist Misunderstanding." *The New York Review of Books*.

Asante, Molefi Kete. 1988. *Afrocentricity*. Trenton, New Jersey: Africa World Press, Inc.

Asante, Molefi Kete. 1987. *The Afrocentric Idea*. Back Flap. Pennsylvania: Temple University Press.

Asante, Molefi Kete. 1990. *Kemet Afrocentricity and Knowledge*. New Jersey: Africa World Press, Inc.

Asante, Molefi Kete. 1990, November. "Battle Over Multicultural Education Rises In Intensity." *Education Week*.

Asante, Molefi Kete. 1991, September. "Putting Africa at the Center." *Newsweek*.

Asante, Molefi Kete. 1992, Summer. "African American Studies: The Future of the Discipline." *The Black Scholar*. Vol. 16. No. 3.

Asante, Molefi Kete. 1996, March. "Reading Race in Antiquity: The Many Fallacies of Mary Lefkowitz." *Black Issues in Higher Education*.

Asante, Molefi Kete. 1996, July/August. "Ancient Truths: New Attacks of Afrocentrism Are As Weak As They Are False." *Emerge*.

Atwater, Deborah, F. 1995. "Asante and the Naming of Names: The Evolution of Rhetorical Concepts." In *Molefi Kete Asante and Afrocentricity: In Praise and Criticism*. Dhyanna Ziegler, Editor. Nashville, Tennessee: Winston Derek Publishing Company.

Auster, Lawrence. 1991, May. "America Is in Danger of Losing its Soul." *Newsday*.

Bernal, Martin. 1987. *Black Athena: The Afroasiatic Roots of Classical Civilization. Volume 1: The Fabrication of Ancient Greece 1785-1985*. New Jersey: Rutgers University Press.

Buchannan, Pat. 1997, July. "Losing America in the Multicultural Mix." *The Washington Times National Weekly Edition*.

Colon, Alan K. 1984. "Critical Issues in Black Studies: A Selective Analysis." *Journal of Negro Education*. Vol. 53. No. 3.

Cooper, Kenneth J. 1992, November 27. "Broadening Horizons: Afrocentrism Takes Root in Atlantic Schools." *The Washington Post*.

Covin, David. 1990, December. "Afrocentricity In O Movimento Negro Unificado." *Journal of Black Studies*. Vol. 21.

D'Souza, Dinesh. 1995. *The End of Racism: Principles For A Multicultural Society*. New York: The Free Press.

Early, Gerald. 1995. "Understanding Afrocentrism: Why Blacks Dream of a World Without Whites." *Civilization*.

Fields, Gary. 1995 September. "Controversy Begins With 'End' of Racism." *USA Today*.

Garland, Sonja D. 1995. "Afrocentricity: Know the Truth of the Past for a Successful Future." In *Molefi Kete Asante and Afrocentricity: In Praise and Criticism*. Dhyana Ziegler, Editor. Nashville, Tennessee: James C. Winston.

Gates, Henry Louis. 1991, September. "Beware of the New Pharaohs." *Newsweek*.

Glazer, Nathan. 1997. *We Are All Multiculturalist Now*. Mass: Harvard University Press.

Hill, Kathleen T. and Hill, Gerald N. 1994. *Real Life Dictionary of American Politics*. Los Angeles: General Publishing Group.

Holloway, Joseph E. 1990. *Africanism in American Culture*. Bloomington and Indianapolis: Indiana University Press.

Hooks, Bell and West, Cornel. 1991. *Breaking Bread: Insurgent Black Intellectual Life*. Boston, Massachusetts: South End Press.

Horwitz, Sari and Loose, Cindy. 1993, September 4. "Afrocentric Program Gets Go-Ahead." *The Washington Post*.

Karenga, Maulana. 1993. *Introduction to Black Studies*. 2nd Edition. Los Angeles, California.

Kershaw, Terry. 1992, Winter. "Afrocentrism and the Afrocentric Method." *The Western Journal of Black Studies*. Vol. 16. No. 3.

Lefkowitz, Mary. 1992, February. "Not Out of Africa: The Origins of Greece and the Illusions of Afrocentrists." *The New Republic*.

Lefkowitz, Mary. 1996. *Not Out of Africa: How Afrocentrism Became An Excuse To Teach Myth As History*. New York: Basic Books.

Leman, N. 1993 January. "Black Nationalism on Campus." *The Atlantic Monthly*.

Magner, Denise K. 1997 April 18. "Deep Rifts Divide Faculty in Temple University's Afrocentric Ph.D. Program." *The Chronicle of Higher Education*.

Mills, David. 1993, August 8. "The West Alternative." *The Washington Post Magazine*.

Monges, Miriam Ma'at-Ka-Re. 1997 June 6. "Africology at Temple University." *The Chronicle of Higher Education.*

Rogers, MacLean. 1994, August/September. "Racism, and Antisemitism in the Classroom." *Midstream.* Vol. 40. No. 6.

Sailer, Steve. 1997, March 10. "Black-to-Back Blacks." *National Review.*

Shea, Christopher. 1997, April 11. "Multiculturalism Gains An Unlikely Supporter." *The Chronicle of Higher Education.*

Shea, Christopher. 1997, May 9. "For These Scholarly Authors, More Is Better: A Few Prolific Professors Take Great Pride in Writing Book After Book." *The Chronicle of Higher Education.*

Sleeper, Jim. 1997. *Liberal Racism.* New York: Viking Penguin.

Specter, Michael. 1990, February 26. "Was Nefertiti Black? Bitter Debate Erupts." *The Washington Post.*

Sundiata, Ibrahim K. 1996, March 22. "The Scholarly Debate Over Afrocentrism." *The Chronicle of Higher Education.*

The Original African Heritage Study Bible. 1993. Nashville, Tennessee: The James C. Winston Publishing Company.

Uriate, Mercedes Lynn de. 1997, September 16. "Lack of Color Becoming A Pattern On University Scene." *Las Vegas Review-Journal.*

Will, George F. 1996, February 19. "Intellectual Segregation." *Newsweek.*

Chapter Six

ଛୋଓଃ

The Politics of Race in Higher Education for African Americans

Education of the Oppressed

At the very outset, it must be clearly understood that "black colleges should never have been necessary" (Waltman, 1994, p. B-1), especially if *all* American citizens had been given an equal chance, or *equality of opportunity* in higher education. Unfortunately, historically black colleges and universities were established not only to educate, but they served as a means to an end for African American students. Therefore, black institutions were/are devoted to African Americans and their educational experiences, and they have been *unparalleled* in their performance in educating the increasing black student population. Elizabeth Culotta (1992, p. 1216), furthermore, states:

> Founded as schools for freed slaves, the historically black colleges and universities (HBCUs) have already evolved through several cycles of change. Throughout this century, while major universities barred their doors, the HBCUs trained blacks to serve as physicians, teachers, and ministers. Finally, the Civil Rights movement expanded job and educational opportunities, black universities broadened their fields, and blacks flocked to majority schools.

Unfortunately, over the years there have been many distortions and mis-statements about the continuing existence of black colleges and universities. Indeed, many believe that black colleges and universities are not viable or necessary; or that they should respond to every single crisis which relates to racial or racist attitudes and situations; but this would be almost impossible, given their limited resources. The economics of black schools of higher education remains a problem, however, and has created turbulence within and outside the academia. In point of fact, and "as many of these institutions pass into the second century of their existence, they are being buffeted by a stormy economy, by the desperate need to upgrade and modernize aging facilities, and by the resistance of local legislators to call for a more equitable distribution of tax-payer dollars between state-supported historically Black and predominantly White institutions" (Whitaker, 1992, p. p. 112). This, of course, is a political issue, and its unlikely to be dismissed any time soon.

It was assumed or hoped that Black colleges and universities would automatically fold or become part of the larger State education systems once integration and desegregation were realized or established. But this never happened. In fact, many needy black institutions are in trouble and are hanging in the balance, while fighting to survive. According to journalist Charles Whitaker (1992, p. 117), "it is universally agreed that if those Black institutions tottering on the brink are to survive into the next century, they will need the financial and emotional backing of Black alumni and friends." And herein lies the political problem with the stability of black institutions. Many HBCUs will continue to be financially strapped. Further, some black colleges and universities have not taken more serious steps to insure their effectiveness and survivability.

For example, and on perhaps a more ominous note, predominantly black Selma University in Alabama is finding it difficult to keep its doors opened, and may lose its full accreditation – and perhaps one day, it might even close. Why? Mostly because of money or funding, and the fact that Selma University cannot pay its debts. Nonetheless, as Joye Mercer (1996, p. A-32) tells us:

> Money has become a concern for much of Selma's history. The university, which has never been flush, was founded shortly after the Civil War as a two-year college to train Baptists for the pulpit. While the campus has enough room for 500 students, its enrollment has fallen off over the past few years, leading to an array of financial problems. Administrators and trustees attribute the decline to publicity about the

university's fiscal woes, its inability to provide more financial aid to students, and its difficulties in raising money.

The financial woes faced by Selma University are not the exception, as there are many other historically black institutions with the same or similar problems. Mercer (1996, p. A-32), however, later notes that "Selma was unaccredited through most of its history, and still managed to survive." Therefore, the *onus* for the survival of these colleges will be on those who have a stake in the institution, as "many historically black colleges do not attract enough individual gifts to support their budgets and must rely heavily on money from tuition, state and federal governments, an affiliated church, or the United Negro College Fund" (Nicklin, 1993, p. A-25).

Additionally, and in an important and far-ranging assessment of American higher education by a panel of public and private university officials and corporate executives, we find that "the nation's colleges and universities need to cut costs dramatically or face a shortfall of funds that will increasingly shut out [blacks and] the poor from higher education and from economic opportunity as well" (Applebome 1997, p. 1). Furthermore, and as Linda Darling-Hammond (1998, p. 28) writes:

> Educational outcomes for minority children are much more a function of their unequal access to key educational resources, including skilled teachers and quality curriculum, than they are a function of race. In fact, the U.S. educational system is one of the most unequal in the industrial world, and students routinely receive dramatically different learning opportunities based on their social status.

All along, of course, we have been aware of these unfair and educational inconsistencies, or practices, and it has been hard for many African-Americans to enjoy the full benefits of education and their American citizenship. And while it is clear from the above passage that there are still educational disparities, it would perhaps take years to correct or reverse these inequities that have long existed between black and white students and institutions. Professor Claude M. Steele (1992, p. 70) has appropriately written:

> Black Americans have had, and continue to have, more than their share [of unfairness]: a history of slavery, segregation, and job ceilings; continued lack of economic opportunity; poor schools; and the related problems of broken families, drug-infested communities, and social

isolation. Any of these factors – alone, in combination, or through accumulated effects – can undermine school achievement. Some analysts point also to black American culture, suggesting that, hampered by disadvantage, it doesn't sustain the values and expectations critical to education, or that it fosters learning orientations ill suited to school achievement, or that it even "opposes" mainstream achievement.

Why are these issues important to black Americans? Perhaps because these are *over-arching* issues that will determine when and what black colleges and universities will close permanently one day. Where young black people are educated is also significant. It may also be of interest to remark that *politicizing* education has always been a reality with politicians in the United States. However, it is perhaps not healthy or reasonable to expect politics and education to mix in any definable way. But for much of this century, politicians and academic educators have concerned themselves almost *exclusively* with this issue. Perhaps for political leverage or some other advantage. Toward this end, and as College President and distinguished educator, Leon Botstein (1997, p. 21) has written:

> In America, education and politics have historically made bad bedfellows. Few issues are raised as often with so few positive results. In the first place, the tenure of most politicians is not long enough for them to be judged by what they might accomplished or fail to do in education. Second, the current political rhetoric concerning education is mired in banalities. Politicians share with most of today's citizens who went to school an instinctive sense of expertise, regardless of whether they did well, poorly, or dropped out, marked by an almost inexhaustible supply of prescription based upon limited and selective *remembrances*.

Bolstein's somewhat startling frankness about politics and education further gives us an understanding of the particular subject in this chapter. Discussions of the politics of education, nonetheless, must not take place in a vacuum, especially when considering black institutions of higher learning and educating African American students. Meanwhile, and not surprisingly, higher education is becoming increasingly crucial for African Americans to achieve economic advancement, no matter if *equality of opportunity* is not achieved. Moreover, some criticisms about many black institutions remain unusually harsh, as they strive for prestige and the limits of their academic possibilities.

Equally important, *everyone* concerned with today's education systems, and how we teach our students, must recognize that, "to equalize the opportunities for higher education among American youth, especially the Negroes who, since the earliest days of the Republic" (McGrath 1965, p. 29) have not been able to have full access to a higher education.

For black students, and despite the concerns already expressed, "the attainment of the baccalaureate degree is arguably the most consistent measure of success in collegiate participation" (Wilson 1992, p. 79). Accordingly, "the idea persists that the college years are crucial, since they prepare an elite to exercise leadership in society" (Botstein 1997, p. 178). Moreover, this interest in education permits us to have a new understanding about black institutions, which is "the last link in the chain of general education, where the purpose of education legitimately reach beyond the narrow but crucial objective of preparing a young [black] person for work and employment" (Botstein 1997, p. 183).

Admittedly, it was in good faith that black colleges were established originally to educate black men and women in the United States for leadership in the mostly black community. Hence, trying to understand the plight and continuation of black colleges and universities is more timely than ever, and now that many white institutions are closing their doors (so to speak) to many African American students. Indeed, there has been a precipitous decline in admissions of African American students at these white institutions because many are not *receptive* to diversity and *parity* toward minority students today. Furthermore, many of these predominantly white universities are divisive, polarizing and politically fraught arenas. The fact is, many white institutions of higher education in the United States do not do a very good job of teaching many black students. Also, according to Elizabeth Janice (1992, p. 26), white colleges and universities are not doing what they can and should do in terms of insuring black students graduate from college. And although the current level of college preparation for African American students may be unacceptable, black institutions are graduating blacks in record numbers.

Equally importantly, and perhaps because of Proposition 209 and the University of California's recent decision to eliminate the use of race preferences in admission to elite campuses (as well as at other white institutions) has cause many historically black institutions to step up their recruiting efforts of black students (Black Colleges . . . 1997, p. 68). Surprisingly, the college enrollment rates at black colleges and universities are soaring as many black students embrace a resurgent black

pride movement, or [are] seek [ing a] more affordable education"
(Sheppard 1994, p. 36).

One must also bear in mind, however, that "enrollments at black
colleges slipped from 234, 000 in 1986, a period during which many
traditionally white schools recruited minority students, then began an
upsurge to 240,000 by 1988" (Sheppard 1994, p. 36). At that time,
moreover, educators believed that economics, or the lack of money, not
discrimination was the blame for lagging minority enrollments at most
American Universities (Study Shows More Minority Students . . . 1996,
p. 7-A). A seemingly obvious point here is that black school enrollments
are now exploding at predominantly black colleges and universities. In
point of fact, and "in recent years the entry rate of black students into
college has been accelerating faster than the national norm" (Braddock
1981, p. 319).

Even more significant, black institutions draw from a population that
is disproportionately poor. Furthermore, we should note that "overall
black student enrollment totaled 1,393,000 in 1992, an increase of 58,
000 over 1991 and an all-time high after dipping from 1,107,000 in
1980 to 1,082,000 in 1986. . . ." (Sheppard 1994, p. 36).

Additionally, a report by the American Council on Education pointed
out that although "gaps still exist in higher education between students of
color and their white peers . . . minority student enrollment at U.S.
colleges rose 5 percent in 1994" (Study Shows More Minority Students . . .
1996, p. 7-A).

But no matter how successful the efforts of white universities are in
admissions of African Americans, black students are likely to make up
the entire population of these historically black colleges and universities
in the near future. And as long as "hostile environments" exist and
persist at predominantly white institutions, black students will continue
to flock to black colleges and universities. This point, of course, is also
important to understand because ". . . boards of higher education, which
used to operate explicitly segregated institutions, face an almost impossible
situation when it comes to expunging suspicion of racism. Even when
race [and politics] does not figure [prominently] in [an educational]
decision, doubt always exists, poisoning the atmosphere and making
rational discussion all but impossible" (Waltman 1994, p. B-1).

Furthermore, some black institutions provide a sheltered environment,
protecting these sometimes vulnerable and "at-risks" black students from
the racial vagaries of life. Moreover, partly in response to this new

population of students at black colleges, there seems to be a limited number of exceptional (or qualified) black and minority students to go around. Of course, "black students on today's campuses may experience far less overt prejudice than their 1950s counterparts but, ironically, [they] may [still] be more racially vulnerable" (Steele 1992, p. 70). Therefore, many black students are opting not to attend traditional white universities, even when they can, and even when actively approached or recruited. On the other hand, and as one might imagine, to attend these black institutions is to have a realistic view of the world, or the society that awaits them. According to Ursula Wagener and Edgar E. Smith (1993, p. 42):

> This upsurge in popularity and visibility has affirmed the claimed special role of HBIs [Historically Black Institutions] in producing leaders. While these institutions enroll only 20 percent of the nation's African American undergraduates, they produce more than a third of its black college graduates. From 1986 to 1990, of the top 10 U.S. baccalaureate institutions that sent Africans on to graduate school and to receive doctorates, nine were HBIs.

It is not surprising, therefore, that Black colleges and universities have played a courageous and historic role in the (righteous) struggle for blacks to achieve an educational opportunity in higher education, as well as having a historical and cultural importance to the black community. This view for black colleges (and institutions) is exceedingly instructive, especially if one recognizes that: Black universities provide perhaps the only means for some African American students to attend college, to succeed, and to acquire an advance degree. Without such colleges and universities, our nation would definitely be the lesser – or worst – especially since many of our accomplished black professionals have graduated from these black colleges and universities (Waltman 1994, p. B-1).

In line with these facts, there is a need to maintain and nurture African American students at these important institutions; and to teach them realistic expectations of the world around them. We must never lose track of the fact that in the recent past, black institutions often felt that they would automatically get the enrollment of *all* qualified and college-bound students. However, this deceptively neat assumption attributed to their decline in black student population in the 1970s and early 1980s. In fact, when this dwindling pool of black students almost dried-up, black colleges and universities became increasingly frustrated with the ideals and principles behind integration. And what this really told us was – black schools were (for a while) becoming increasingly complacent and content with the *status quo*. But on educational politics, and especially when discussing black colleges and universities, it becomes very accommodating to suggest:

> As the predominantly Negro colleges and universities rise to the challenges of the coming years, they will need advice and assistance in dealing with a great variety of problems such as their changing purposes in the light of social evolution, their educational programs, the kind and quality of their faculties, the size and character of their student bodies, the source and magnitude of their financial support, the size and character of their physical plants, and a host of other problems with which they, even more than other institutions of higher education, will be afflicted (McGrath 1965, p. 161).

The educational environment at black institutions, however, is pragmatic in that these colleges and universities are now creating opportunities for blacks to expand their intellectual horizons, which give black institutions the *ammunition* for their preservation. More importantly, as Gregory Kannerstein (1978, p. 29) tells us, "Black colleges [have] provided valuable perspectives on American education and society." But these important contributions are not without their critics and weaknesses, as many claim that there is a danger in so-called coddling black students in that "campuses devoted to nurturing may not be as academically rigorous as majority universities that expect students to "sink or swim" (Culotta 1992, p. 1218).

But one must ask the question: How does education actually influence the behavior of black students? Yes, some potential black students are woefully unprepared for college life, and often lack an adequate grade-point, or high-school average. Nevertheless, many of our educators have little knowledge about what it takes to be successful in college, especially the 'nuts-and-bolts' required to study and make the coveted grade. They also have a glamorized version of what it means to have a college life, as well as the lack of tenacity, motivation, and for some, the commitment to complete the requirements for graduation. According to Professor Claude M. Steele (1992, p. 70), "70 percent of all black students who enroll in four-year colleges drop out at some point, compared with 45 percent of whites. [And] at any given time nearly as many black males are incarcerated as are in college in this country."

Furthermore, many educators and critics believe that the black student's educational experiences will be diminished by a less heterogenous atmosphere, which does not reflect the society beyond the campus. But we must also recognize or understand that many educators and university officials are not agonizing over the threat to the multicultural complexion of the various campuses. But to add to these realistic and important issues, we must also be cognizant that "the education of African American college students is . . . a national issue" (Waltman 1994, p. B-1). The difficult *truth* is that, given the current state of our education, and –

> As far as disadvantaged Negro and other youth are concerned, the concept of [educational] excellence can be realized, not by the application of the negative philosophy of casting out all those who do not come up to elitist standards – and this view appears to be gaining popularity among many American educators – but by taking students where they are socially, economically, and educationally, and developing their abilities to the fullest (McGrath 1965, pp. 9-10).

School Segregation Revisited

Black institutions, of course, fit this bill. A key concern, again, is whether black colleges and universities will be able to keep their direction and place in educational policies in the face of "escalating political pressure" from those who would like to see them disband and close their doors permanently. Under these circumstances, for example, and "in the domain of state-supported historically black institutions, the battle for equitable funding has reached the Supreme Court in the form of *Ayers v. Mabus*" (Whitaker 1992, p. 117). The purpose of this 20-year-old case was to "change forever the way States view[ed] and fund[ed] Black institutions in their purview" (Whitaker 1992, p. 117).

All the same, there is something more that should be said about the *Ayers* case, which "maintain that a dual system of funding has purposely kept Black institutions from competing on equal footing with their White counterparts. . . . [And] as a remedy, [it was proposed] that the States provide corrective funding that would enhance the academic offerings, buildings and facilities of historically Black institutions" (Whitaker 1992, p. 116). And, if you look at it critically, perhaps this would redress the past discriminatory policies States had toward black universities, which they often thought were inadequate schools.

It is important, however, that we not draw the wrong conclusions about the *Ayers* case and the many points of contention between the two very different higher educational school systems, such as the obvious financial gaps and divergence of interests and ideas that exist among these educational organizations. Equally worrisome is having a supposedly separate-but-equal black and white, higher educational school systems again, which is clearly a step backward. But we must also bear in mind that because of the way the various State higher educational school systems are set up, we are perhaps unwilling to *truly* give parity to these two institutional organizations, or make black colleges and universities a part of the entire educational spectrum.

Ultimately, we must ask: Is it desirable for us not to educate our black youth in American society in any educational forum? Indeed, how do we improve inadequate Black colleges and universities if we abolish Affirmative Action admissions at the top schools? Even more important, how do we insure Black institutions are considered when recruiting for important government jobs? An Office of Personnel Management (OPM) study, for instance, showed that "federal agencies have not recruited on HBCU campuses . . . [and the lack of recruitment] couple with the students' stated lack of awareness of other federal employment information sources have created a tremendous void in the federal recruiting pipeline" (Brown 1992, p. 29).

The government's position on this matter, I believe is demonstrably wrong, as many of things we have discussed in this chapter. Nonetheless, quite a few of these black institutions are growing substantially and are forging their own paths toward business success rather than waiting for monetary "hand-outs" from education-related charities, philanthropists, and those sympathetic to the cause of education for blacks, which come too infrequently. Still, many politicians and educators believe that black colleges and universities are so strong that they can withstand *any* pressure to fold and go away. This tenaciousness has helped to make black schools distinctive institutions in themselves. However, because of mainly poor finances, "officials of black colleges say it is especially important that the smaller, lesser-known black institutions solve their [questionable management decisions and oversight by their trustees]" (Nicklin 1993, p. 25). Furthermore, many black colleges and universities are becoming more politically astute and business-oriented or *driven*, as they "continue to survive," and where we find that "most college graduates who are black still receive their degrees from the schools that are classified as "historically black" (Browning and Williams 1978, p. 92).

Such effectiveness might also lead one to ask: Should black institutions put their own interest above some overall nationalistic or national mythic goal of integration? Indeed, what will be the educational opportunities and return for blacks? In the long run, as the late and famous Dr. Benjamin Mays warned, Black colleges and universities should not "apologize for their existence, to become weak-kneed, to stop striving for excellence, and to stop trying to raise money for their support" (Willie and Edmonds 1978, p. 26). And this, in turn, will sustain the importance black colleges and universities need to play in contemporary life in the United States. According to Mays, "if America allows black colleges to die, it will be the worst kind of discrimination and denigration known in history. To decree that colleges born to serve Negroes are not worthy of surviving now would be damnable act" (Willie and Edmonds 1978, p. 27). All this says is: destroying Black colleges and universities would also have an enormous *negative* impact on the nation's social fabric. According to conservative economist and columnist, Thomas Sowell (1993, p. 303):

> All the ingredients for a successful educational system already exist in the United States – some of the leading scholars in the world in numerous fields, masses of college educated people capable of teaching . . . and a public whose willingness to buckle down to the task of teaching academic skills to the next generation. The problems are fundamentally institutional. Changing those institutions is the key to changing behavior and attitudes too long insulated from accountability.

One historical note should be pointed out to those carping about eliminating Black colleges and universities – that is, without these venerable black institutions, many African Americans would be uneducated, and have no access to positions of influence, wealth and power. And in the final analysis, as Professor Glazer, a former "academic opponent of Affirmative Action," has stated, this exclusion "would undermine the legitimacy of American democracy" (Lewis 1998, p. A-23).

Despite words to the contrary, black universities were founded to serve the many black communities where they are located, specifically in the South. This is important to note here because, "although historically black colleges and universities have tried to distance themselves from the problems of the communities where they are actually located, "viewing

the blight and crime as a barrier to the success of the institution," many
are now realizing that "they have to work in tandem with the community"
(Walker 1997, p. A-31). In other words, they serve the poor, inner-city
areas in which they were established, and by "strategic planning, with
the result of a stronger image and greater community support" (Wagener
and Smith 1993, p. 49), Black institutions will continue to survive, and
thrive no matter the circumstances. This means that along with available
facilities, classrooms and all the other appurtenances of a university, "a
supportive community [will] provide opportunities for friendships outside
the class room, including those with teachers and staff members. It [will]
also provide students with opportunities to participate in campus life and
to rehearse for roles to be assumed in society, generating the esteem that
comes from being recognized" (Wagener and Smith 1993, p. 42).

   We must all share a common concern about the future prospects for
black colleges and universities, because ultimately, and

> perhaps the greatest and most distinctive contribution of black colleges
> to the American philosophy of higher education has been to emphasize
> and legitimate public and community service as a major objective of
> colleges and universities. The most superficial perusal of the catalogs
> and other publications of these colleges reveals how deeply ingrained
> this mission is in their consciousness. Enter to learn; go forth to serve
> is a common motto. Service is invariably linked with instruction,
> research, and learning in descriptions by the colleges of their principal
> functions (Kannerstein 1978, p. 31).

   Perhaps the most important assets black colleges and universities can
provide are: they develop leaders, giving young blacks the confidence to
compete in our complex and modern cosmopolitan world; and they
graduate more African Americans than any other schools. In 1992, for
example, "the nation's top five schools that award bachelor degrees to
African Americans [were] all HBCUs: Howard University [744 students],
Southern University Agricultural and Mechanical College [575 students],
Hampton University [539 students], North Carolina Agricultural and
Technical State University [509 students], and Jackson State University
[463 students]" (Janice 1992, p. 26).

   Therefore, despite their deficiencies, and mainly poor finances, many
apparently are surviving, and conducting the business of higher education.
In fact, many of these Black institutions are being *reshaped* and
transformed for the betterment of all America. However, many educators

and "black researchers [believe] that if the black universities truly want to achieve success [especially] in research, then many will need new leadership, since today's administrators may not have the research backgrounds themselves to understand what's needed" (Culotta 1992, pp. 1223-1224).

Given the above statistics and beliefs, and as one can perhaps ascertain, the demand for higher education in America, generally among Blacks, is still great, insurmountable. Toward this end, however, one must understand that colleges and universities in particular:

> are flooded with progressive experiments and social agendas that either crash in flames or crowd out actual learning – whole language instruction, cooperative learning, the politics of identity, outcome-based education, history as group therapy. An emphasis on egalitarianism in the classroom often has strange effects, making some teacher suspicious of achievement and any knowledge that 'contributes to inequality' (Leo 1998, p. 4-E).

In another vein, and typically, black students represent the first in their families to attend college. Even more important, the equality of opportunity in higher education for blacks will continue to be a political and national concern. For instance, "an amendment that would have cut off Federal aid to any public college or university that considered race, ethnicity or gender in its admissions process" was recently defeated in the House in Congress "by a vote of 249 to 171" (Lewis 1998, p. A-23). Essentially, and according to Journalist Anthony Lewis (1998, p. A-23):

> That vote may have been a turning point in the struggle over affirmative action in higher education. The issue could not have been more squarely presented. The amendment would have forced an end to affirmative action, and slashed the numbers of minority students at the country's premier public universities.

Therefore, many black students are finding disheartening experiences at predominantly white institutions by the obstacles created by racism and discrimination; hence, they are retreating to Black institutions. Indeed, many African Americans feel betrayed by several of these top white schools' recent (and so-called) 'race-blind' approach to admissions, an issue which has been *catapulted* into the national and political spotlight. However, the thing to remember about black students attending predominantly black colleges and universities is: they (black schools) provide the *catalyst* for them to do great things. Perhaps needless to add, as Professor Earl J. McGrath (1965, p. 8) has pointed out:

> American history testifies abundantly to the fact that these [black] students have often achieved positions of high status in their occupations and in public life generally. The hard fact remains that unless relatively inexpensive higher education is near at hand, the majority of these young people will not be able to continue their formal schooling beyond high school. Hence, as many as possible of the existing colleges should be preserved while strenuous efforts are made to improve them.

Conclusions

From the educator's perspective, a high percentage of black institutions lack the political *savvy* to become something more than they are today – that is, full-fledge universities with many renown educational departments, faculty members, and professional schools. However, the political *overtones* of their existence are tremendous – such as: Can we ultimately solve these vital Black institutions' financial and educational problems? Writing about the crisis of higher education, Neil Postman (1996, pp. 119-120) states:

> We may have insufficient facts to support an idea; or some of the facts we have may be incorrect, perhaps generated by a festering emotion; or the conclusions we have drawn may not be entirely logical; or some definition we are employing may not be applicable; or we may be merely repeating an idea we have heard expressed by some authority and have not examined its implications carefully (Postman 1996, pp. 119-120).

Black colleges and universities, in this sense, give us an impressive picture of how higher educational institutions must develop, adapt, and survive. Fortunately, their survival will be a constant impediment to their overall transformation and development. One must also bear in mind that educational failures at these schools are expensive, and the expense is translated into poorly educated students.

Nevertheless, it is possible, of course, that black educational institutions will survive the test of time, as they occupy a distinctive *niche* in American higher education. And in the ultimate consideration and analysis, "whatever route individual black colleges might take, the decisions should be made by people whose first and only priority is the well-being of those institutions" (Waltman 1994, p. B-2). Lastly, and as we have seen, the major source of political controversy, regarding black American colleges in the past and in the immediate future, *will be about their survival!*

References

Applebome, Peter. 1997, June 18. "Rising College Costs Imperil the Nation, Blunt Report Says." *The New York Times*.

"Black Colleges Step-up Recruitment." 1997, February 17. *Las Vegas Review-Journal*.

Botstein, Leon. 1997. *Jefferson's Children: Education and the Promise of American Culture*. New York: Doubleday.

Braddock II, Henry, Jomils and Dawkins, Marvin P. 1981. "Predicting Black Academics In Higher Education." *The Journal of Negro Education*. Vol. 50. No. 3.

Brown, Luther. 1992, October. "Recruits At HBCUs." *Black Enterprise*.

Browning, Smith, Jane E. and Williams, John B. 1978. "History and Goals of Black Institutions of Higher Learning." in *Black Colleges in America: Challenge, Development, Survival*. Charles V. Willie and Ronald E. Edmonds, editors. Teachers College, Columbia University, New York: Teachers College Press.

Culotta, Elizabeth. 1992, November 13. "Black Colleges Cultivate Scientists." *Science*. Vol. 258.

Darling-Hammond, Linda. 1998, Spring. "Unequal Opportunity: Race and Education." *Brookings Review*. Vol. 16. No. 2.

Janice, Elizabeth. 1992, August. "1st in Black Degrees." *Black Enterprise*.

Kannerstein, Gregory. 1978. "Black Colleges: Self-Concept," in *Black Colleges in America: Challenge, Development Survival*. Charles V. Willie and Ronald R. Edmonds, editors. Teachers College, Columbia University, New York: Teachers College Press.

Lewis, Anthony. 1998, May 18. "Turn of the Tide." *The New York Times*.

Leo, John. 1998. "Blame For Low Test Scores Rests Directly With School Methods." *Las Vegas Review-Journal*.

McGrath, Earl J. 1965. *The Predominantly Negro Colleges and Universities in Transition*. Teacher College, Columbia University: Bureau of Publications.

Mays, Benjamin E. 1978. "The Black College in Higher Education," in *Black Colleges in America: Challenge, Development, Survival*. Charles V. Willie and Ronald R. Edmonds, editors. Teachers College, Columbia University, New York: Teachers College Press.

Mercer, Joye. 1996, April 12. "A Struggling Campus Turns to Prayer." *The Chronicle of Higher Education*.

Nicklin, Julie L. 1993, March 10. "Financial Troubles at Small Black Colleges Raise Questions About Role of Their Trustees in Overseeing Management." *The Chronicle of Higher Education*.

Postman, Neil. 1996. *The End of Education: Redefining The Value of School*. New York: Alfred A. Knopf.

Sheppard, Nathaniel, Jr. 1994, July 24. "Black College Enrollments Soar on Pride." *Pacific Stars and Stripes*.

Sowell, Thomas. 1993. *Inside American Education: The Decline, The Deception, The Dogmas*. New York: The Free Press.

Steele, Claude M. 1992, April. "Race and the Schooling of Black Americans." *The Atlantic Monthly*.

"Study Shows More Minority Students Enrolling in College." 1996, June 10. *Las Vegas Review-Journal*.

Wagener, Ursula and Smith, Edgar E. 1993, January/February. "Maintaining A Competitive Edge: Strategic Planning for Historically Black Institutions." *Change*.

Walker, Paulette. 1997, June 13. "Black Colleges Help Revive Struggling Neighborhoods." *The Chronicle of Higher Education*.

Waltman, Jerold. 1994, July 6. "Assuring the Future of Black Colleges." *The Chronicle of Higher Education*.

Whitaker, Charles. 1992, March. "Black Colleges At the Crossroads." *Ebony*.

Wilson, Reginald. 1992, Spring. Book review of *Fostering Minority Access and Achievement in Higher Education*. San Francisco: Jossey-Bass, 1987, by Richard C. Richardson, in *Harvard Educational Review*. Vol. 62. No. 1.

Chapter Seven

ℰᎧᏇ

The Future of Black Colleges and Universities in the United States

The Need for Black Higher Educational Institutions

There has been a struggle within Black colleges and universities over the question of how one defines the so-called black institutions of higher education. Toward this end, Julie A. Reuben (1996, p. 10) writes that, "The traditional account of the history of higher education emphasizes a revolution in the late nineteenth century. [And] according to this historical model, true higher education did not exist in the United States until the development of the modern university" (Reuben 1996, p. 10).

We should not make too much of this idea; however, all this is important to understand because as most United States histories have already established, "the founding of black colleges, although made possible by white philanthropy, represented a continuation of black interest in education . . ." (Allen 1974, p. 2). Consequently, we must ask the question of whether the repeal of racial preferences will change the face of the American campus or university in the United States. Perhaps it will. Or it might create once again white bastions of educational institutions. Moreover, is the pace of higher educational school reform *too* slow? Should there be, for example, tax cuts for black colleges and universities, public and private, and increases in federal grants to make these institutions viable and more affordable?

Another valid question is: Are many black students less qualified than whites for admission to prestigious and selective white universities? Moreover, if standardized test scores dominate the admission process, would this mean a total elimination of African American students from white colleges and universities in the United States?

From the outset, then, it must be understood that white and black colleges and universities are not equal, or they are not necessarily the same. What do we mean by this? Besides not being uniform in quality, black schools have never had the prestige and power most of their white counterparts have had. Nor have some black colleges been able to integrate teaching and educational research. Professor of political science at the University of Southern Mississippi, Jerold Waltman (1994, p. B1), would agree with this contention, because he writes:

> Public historically black colleges always have been treated as if they were second-rate, if not third-rate, institutions. Corners were cut in construction, maintenance was woefully inadequate, salaries were abysmally low, libraries were severely understocked. The institutions were neglected and disdained.

Nonetheless, many black institutions, like Howard University, Fisk, Morehouse and Atlanta have become first-rate schools and traditional research universities, despite the odds. Therefore, does this mean black schools of higher education are more responsive to their black students' varying abilities and needs?

Whatever we may think of such an assertion, it goes without saying, blacks "since the earliest days of the Republic, through neglect, [racism], and discrimination have been denied full access to higher education" (McGrath, 1965, p. 29). Furthermore, and nevertheless, black colleges and universities are still the African American's opportunity for higher education. According to professor Mack Jones (1971, p. 736), black colleges have been used as an instrument in the African American struggle to achieve equal status in the United States. And this, of course, has come with a significant, emotional and financial price. Jones (1971, p. 736) goes on to accurately write:

> Black were largely illiterate, impoverished political subjects without political rights, whose claim to citizenship and, indeed, membership

in the human family were questioned by the society in which they lived.

Similarly, the African Americans' so-called need for education was also questioned, and in some cases, flat-out denied. It had been generally assumed by the (white) dominate culture that blacks were sub-human and uneducable. However, many blacks (in the past and especially today) see higher-education as the gateway to becoming a part of America's middle classes, and to a secured future. Equally important, and prior to the nineteen sixties, black colleges provided all of the educational opportunities for aspiring black college students. However, with the desegregation of all American higher educational institutions, there has been serious concern about the *necessity* or *value* of black colleges and universities (Anderson and Hrabowski 1977, p. 295). Indeed, the future of Black universities and colleges is *inextricably* tied to past and present political and educational battles. It was, for example, even reasonable to assume back in the 1960s that there was "abundant evidence that the public mind and conscience [were] aroused to the absolute social and moral necessity of improving educational opportunities for Negro [or Black] youth" (McGrath 1965, p. vi). Current indicators, however, have proven the opposite of this past approach or assumption.

Be that as it may, we must note that "propositions that blacks are educable and that higher education should be made available to them have been firmly established and doctrines of racial inferiority have been debunked in spite of efforts to resurrect them" (Jones 1971, p. 739). Generally speaking, an adequate educational opportunity means:

> Higher education should be as universally available as possible. That is, there should be higher education at low cost (federally and state financed) for very large sectors of the relevant age-grade. Behind this suggestion is the explicit desire to draw into higher education many lower-class and minority young. It is hoped that such a policy would reduce the opportunity gap between the middle and lower classes attending colleges and would ameliorate the accumulative disadvantage of poverty and cultural deprivation (Parsons and Platt 1973, p. 200).

Interestingly enough, there are some educators and academics who do not believe or regard black colleges and universities as being completely necessary. Some critics, moreover, would suggest that many of these black colleges and universities are only advanced secondary or second-rate schools masquerading as universities. That is not important. How these schools regard themselves is what is important. Hence, they must acknowledge without hesitation that even though there are differences from white universities, they too are vital to the educational system in America, or the United States.

Therefore, can the opportunities for higher education be equalized? It first must be understood that "the nation's predominantly Negro colleges are located in a wide area stretching from Pennsylvania to Texas across the border and southern states" (McGrath 1965, p. 30). But can they compete successfully with their white counterparts? Although an increasing number of critics and detractors insist that black institutions do not play a significant part in the overall American higher educational system, we must also be cognizant that,

> All but a handful of the predominantly Negro colleges are located in the former segregating states. By law and by custom, enrollment has been and continues to be predominantly – almost exclusively – uni-racial. And within these all-black institutions, the underlying assumptions of American higher education in general have been accepted. Just as in the formerly all-white institutions, so in the black colleges, the aims are: to acquaint the student with the mainstream of western civilization, to afford opportunity for self-discovery and maturity in terms of middle class values, and to insure the professional competence to "make it" in a white man's world (Gallagher 1971, p. 32).

Black colleges and universities, however, have complex and sometimes apparently contradictory educational goals and aspirations. Moreover, are these black schools failing to equip black students for the demands of our democracy, given that they are becoming increasingly populated because of black enrollments? After all, and of course, admittedly, "the purpose of education is to give the student the intellectual tools to analyze, whether verbally or numerically, and to reach conclusions based on logic and conclusions based on logic and evidence. [However], the attempts of schools and colleges to encompass far more than they can handle are an important part of the reason why they are handling education so poorly" (Sowell 1993, p. 18).

Furthermore, critics like the black economist and conservative newspaper columnist, Thomas Sowell, would perhaps say that many black students are not prepared, or do not have the inclination, aptitude or right attitudes for going on to college, so maybe they shouldn't even try? But black students who may lack the necessary skills to be fully competitive and productive as college students could perhaps benefit from attending a predominantly black institute. But what happens to the less academic black students? There have been studies that proclaim that "the relatively poor performance of [Black students] can be interpreted as an effect of personal threat experienced in the biracial [education] situations" (Katz and Greenbaum 1963, pp. 562) at most predominantly white colleges. So can we assume as the political and civil rights activist, Vernon Jordan (1975, p. 163) asserts:

> Black students on white campuses are victims of destructive myths that often distort the degree of alienation and separatism that exists. The typical picture of the black student as being an angry militant refusing all contact with whites and obsessed with his black studies courses. . . .

In point of fact, and in the academic environment, "the foremost challenge to predominantly white institutions of higher learning is to evaluate carefully and to reconsider those admissions policies of many years' standing in order to provide *all* segments of our society with an opportunity to share in programs of higher education" (Green 1969, p. 910). But can we truly have a race-blind policy in school admissions? More importantly, will dropping race and gender preferences in admissions solve the education problems in America? Why is all this important? Isn't it more appropriate for *any* and *all* students to receive their higher education at the college of their choice? Or is it conceivable that black students will always have to attend institutions largely made up of blacks in segregated black communities? All in all, and quite appropriately, "Institutions of higher learning, along with other socialization agents are responsible for insuring that patterns of behavior dictated by the [dominate] regime are accepted as legitimate" (Jones 1971, p. 732). More importantly, and alternatively, can predominantly white universities tailor more of their courses or their curricula to the needs of black students? Another important consideration is what activities will take place after Affirmative Action has been completely eliminated (if ever) at white institutions. For the moment, however, we must be concerned with a different issue. That is, since blacks, in the past, have been systematically discriminated against in higher education, perhaps "colleges and universities should also be asking: How may campuses become qualified to serve the needs of black students? This question needs to be [addressed] and asked on all campuses – both the so-called predominantly white and the so-called predominantly black" (Gallagher 1971, p. 32).

Indeed, should we allow black students time to correct their deficiencies (if any) at these institutions? Clearly, can we say that all black students are uneducable or inadequately prepared? And what part can black institutions play in helping and encouraging these [at risk] students? Although black schools share a great deal with white universities, they are designed to enable black students to concentrate on their core responsibilities, such as getting an adequate education and being able to compete with other white universities. We must also recognize that, "Historically, black colleges have been pressured to conform to values and curricula imposed on them from the larger society. It should be of little wonder, then, that residual conformist or over conformist tendencies remain" (Fleming, 1984, p. 154).

To this day, however, black colleges and universities have been one of the most influential organizations in the black community. Of course, we should also take note that "Black colleges afford more opportunities for black students to assume leadership roles in extracurricular activities, thereby providing them with a rehearsal for the roles they are expected to assume in society. This kind of experience offers some of the informal learning that is an essential part of the educational process" (Fleming, 1984, p. 152). According to professor Mack Jones (1971, pp. 741-742), black colleges and universities offer another important advantage, as they:

> have the power to remake the political consciousness of the black student and ultimately of the black nation. That is their primary responsibility to the larger black community. If it is met, secondary responsibilities such as working with community politics, providing staff assistance for community leaders, and so on will take care of themselves.

As a consequence, can predominantly black colleges and universities be matched with predominantly white institutions? Or can they keep up with the technological advancements in higher education? Equally important, can blacks and their institutions acquire the assets necessary to stay competitive with other universities and effectively serve the needs of the black community at the same time? Indeed, what are those things or key factors in attracting new black students, given that:

The increased college enrollment of blacks, particularly in historically white colleges, has raised the question of whether there is a difference in academic achievement between those black students who have attended predominantly white colleges and those who have attended traditionally black colleges at comparable stages in their careers (Anderson and Hrabowski, 1977, p. 294).

Perhaps it is not difficult so far to assess the full impact, role, and contribution of black colleges and universities; therefore, one must ask: how can these institutions become a part of America's new education agenda? It is infuriating to note that "some believe that large numbers of the faculty, members in the predominantly Negro colleges and universities, especially the most accomplished scholars, should be immediately engaged by the white northern colleges and universities; others believe that such a one-way migration would greatly damage the total program of higher education for Negroes" (McGrath 1965, pp. ix-x).

It also should be made unmistakably clear that black institutions make-up only a small part of the American academic spectrum, so are we suggesting they should be limited or eliminated? On the surface, many of these institutions appear to have no problems; however, they are rife with problems or educational and academic concerns, such as their financial survival, and standards of (academic) performance (and excellence). Other factors, nonetheless, have remained just as critical to black colleges and universities' continued success: also their focus on providing both the finest education and professional training. These things, of course, will only be sustained if they survive, or keep their doors opened.

According to a study conducted by the National Association For Equal Opportunity in Higher Education (1978, p. 3):

These special problems have perhaps had negative impact on curricular offerings at these institutions. While white institutions as a group have traditionally provided highly diversified curricula for their students, most black colleges, on the other hand, historically focused on the training of black men and women for careers in teaching, the industrial arts, agriculture, and the ministry, simply because broader employment opportunities were generally denied their graduates.

This profound and informative study goes on to cogently report that "there are those [black] institutions which have traditionally offered professional education programs, but they are in the minority" (NAFEO in Higher Education 1978, p.3). Unfortunately, our race-conscious society has a tendency to place different standards on Black institutions of higher learning. Therefore, are black colleges and universities viewed as a sort of mediocrity of higher education? Even more important, how do we address the current critical needs of Historically Black Colleges and Universities? Furthermore, it has long been asserted that "the question the black colleges have to answer is not how successful they are in relating to high-sounding phrases about education for democracy but specifically how well and how thoroughly they are preparing black youth to grasp the reality of the peculiar brand of democracy in U.S. society" (LeMelle and LeMelle 1969, p. 3).

Black institutions have been able to accomplish this for black students even though they have suffered many indignities and hardships. (And, why can't all black Americans be given a taste of academic life?). It might be argued that, in this sense, black students should be given a university experience that is both fitting (to their abilities), and applicable to their culture, as well as being inexpensive to accommodate those eager for a college degree. Perhaps black educational institutions fit this bill, as they (black students) at black colleges and universities get the best of all worlds by having professors from the entire spectrum of American educational institutions.

Although black students are still subordinated and made marginal within the United States educational context, how can the black student population be included or incorporated into our system of mass higher education?

The Future of Black Institutions

The future of black colleges and universities, of course, are at stake. And perhaps administrators will eventually be able to better familiarize themselves with these institutions and realize their value to our system of higher education. Ultimately, they should recognize that these educational opportunities are necessary. Sadly, and in any event, according to Earl J. McGrath, "some educators think that closing from a third to a half of the predominantly Negro colleges would, more than any other one thing, improve the higher education of Negroes [or blacks]; others . . . believe such an action would be a profound disservice to both the Negro and white youth who constitute their potential student bodies" (McGrath, 1965, p. ix).

I think we should embrace and believe more in the latter course of action. Moreover, I think we must in turn ask the question: How long will two separate systems of higher education exist in America – one for Blacks and one for Whites? Indeed, should the weaker black colleges be eliminated? Or are we condemned to always operate a segregated system of higher education? Furthermore, does the continuation of these black schools perpetuate a dehumanizing myth? That is, do black universities provide academic degrees less in quality to those offered by white universities? Moreover, should poor black students be deterred from embarking on a course of higher education at even black colleges and universities?

There are, to be sure, arguments on both sides as to why they (black schools) should be disbanded. For instance, some conservative educational reformers "believe that admissions standards [at black] institutions, especially the private colleges ought to be rapidly raised to narrowly restrictive levels, and scholarships provided for able but poor students; others . . . believe that such a step would exclude not only many of the poor but also of the potentially able [White and Black] youth who could not meet the higher standards" (McGrath 1965, p. x).

In this view, and to be sure, we must understand critically, and without question, that "to increase the relevance of the [black] university and to make higher education available to a larger and more representative portion of our society, what is needed is not a raising or even a lowering of standards, but instead the use of a different set of standards which takes into account motivational and attitudinal as well as the usual intellectual factor" (Green 1969, p. 910).

There is, of course, a remarkable diverse range of black higher-educational institutions, so how does one set out to broaden the education of all citizens of the United States? It must be certainly known that black colleges and universities have achieved a higher academic standard than ever before, and through no less effort from their dogged ability to survive (and in some cases thrive), despite the inevitable odds. Some would claim that this is some type of neo-separatism, but what we must realize is these black institutions had (and have) no other choice than to be separate. But, more importantly, and at the same time, "these [black] schools were accused of being white colleges in black face, and courses in black history, literature and art were demanded, along with a demand that the black colleges must 'relate' to the local black community" (Allen, 1974, p. 3).

Therefore, given the circumstances, we must ask: How can we preserve and strengthen black institutions? Furthermore, can they [black colleges] be improved? Are they fragile and weak institutions? It is clear that these vibrant schools have unique and definite responsibilities, but "the black colleges are faced with the most difficult job of any educational institution in America. Their task involves both the restoration of the damaged black personality and education of the individual to cope with the realities of black survival in American society" (LeMelle and LeMelle 1969, p. 2). Under these particular circumstances, and as Gallagher (1971, p. 34) cogently explains, "a few of the more than one hundred black institutions have also attempted to build within the student a self-image of dignity and of pride in his blackness, and their graduates have known that black was beautiful long before the slogan was coined." In the ultimate and final analysis, and invariably:

> Black colleges, like all other black institutions, must legitimize themselves in the black community before they will be in a position to compete effectively with white institutions and no longer feel compelled to be like them. This is not a prescription for intellectual isolationism in black higher education. To the contrary, it is a call for greater involvement and interchange of ideas and a more embracing pursuit of knowledge (LeMelle and LeMelle 1969, p. 126).

This legitimization and actualization will be accomplished by constant vigilance and monitoring of these black institutions to ensure that they are in line with our national educational priorities and that there can be a redemption of blacks through education. The business of a substantial number of many black colleges and universities should be to provide a steadying influence and ongoing support and remedial training, if necessary, to black students. Operating under this philosophy, of course, *quality* must be paramount at black schools, since they represent such a broad array of educational goals and differences; hence, *quality* is imperative, and should never be considered a substitute for mediocrity.

Consequently, and in many respects, "the black colleges must respond not only to the blackness of their students but to the great diversity of those students' needs. These students deserve a form of higher education for their real needs in a valid and meaningful context, regardless of how much or how little the style of this education conforms to set and generally alien norms and standards" (LeMelle and LeMelle, 1969, pp. 2-3).

Therefore, predominantly black schools must maintain themselves at the cutting edge, focusing on what they do best, while state and federal governments support and help them operate more efficiently and financially from time to time. The goal and efforts of these black institutions must also be to encourage (always) the black student, especially to graduate. Why is this important? Liberal scholars of education would perhaps say that this is very important. However, as they grapple with the question of why these schools should exist at all, we must also understand that:

Although effective higher education for black Americans will not eliminate entirely the immediate causes of the disparity between black and white (nor will it necessarily eliminate the root cause – discriminatory racism), it will go a long way toward making race less relevant in black/white inter-group relations (LeMelle and LeMelle 1969, pp. 109-110).

The passionate debates of whether these predominantly black colleges and universities should continue to exist (and in the long run) will no doubt persist; and perhaps many under-represented minority students in our society will continue to pursue higher educational degrees. More importantly, if black institutions are not able to survive, it might adversely affect us all indirectly. Hence, particular attention must be paid to the various needs of young, at-risk black students. Indeed, blacks must have education and opportunities at all levels if they are to become productive members of society. Moreover, how can our federal government simultaneously concentrate more money and support to these black institutions for their continuing existence? Paradoxically and ironically, as professors LeMelle and LeMelle (1969, p. 35) conclude: "The question whether or not there will be a continuing need for the black college is now totally irrelevant. Fully transformed, the traditional Negro colleges will contribute even more to the total development of black Americans. The transformation of these colleges into institutions purposefully striving to achieve black relevancy is ultimately dependent upon fundamental changes in the attitudes of black Americans themselves about these institutions."

Furthermore, the so-called "black universities" need to exist, to be there to point out how richly diverse and important they are to the United States' education system. Moreover, will racial differences between these institutions continue? Or what is the *commonality* with other

American institutions? It remains to be seen whether, having achieved a similar status as white universities, black colleges and universities will now feel confident enough to offer more professional education programs, or whether they will aspire to become exactly like their counterparts. Such measures underscore the point that:

> many predominantly white colleges have resources superior to those available at the majority of black colleges, in terms of the number of Ph. D. s on the faculty, the quantity and quality of the library holdings, and the size of the endowment or state appropriation. Because of these superior resources, one might assume that black students who attend white colleges would be more successful in graduate study than those who attend black colleges (Anderson and Hrabowski 1977, p. 295).

Unfortunately, it must be understood that many students who enroll in white universities fail to cope or complete the necessary requirements, and (usually) drop-out after their first year. Furthermore, many of the very best black students are being siphoned or creamed off to white universities. The irony in all this, however, is that, "Despite their poorer resources, black colleges still possess the capacity to permit the expression of natural adolescent motivations for cognitive growth. [And] this appears to be so because the black college environment offers a student a wider network of supportive relationships" (Fleming 1984, pp. 150-151).

If all this is so, moreover, it seems wrong for anyone to speculate about the necessity or future of black colleges and universities. Indeed, it is too simple to conclude that eliminating black institutions will solve our higher education problems or address institutional racism and other educational inequalities (head on) in our society. Nevertheless, "Quality higher education for black Americans continues to be a major issue in higher education" (Anderson and Hrabowski 1977, p. 294).

Which brings us to the central question: Should black students and teachers be held to higher standards if permitted to survive into the millennium? Would this make them better – or will our general education improve? In fact, how can the quality of all educational institutions be improved? According to newspaper columnist John Leo (1998, pp. 1-4), "Largely because of the culture . . . our . . . education is pervaded by social attitudes that work against achievement. One is the heavy emphasis on feelings, subjectivity and self-esteem at the expense of actual learning and thinking."

If Leo is right, perhaps the only way to improve black colleges and universities is to drastically reform the curricular, and raise the academic admissions standards. To this end, it is essential that there is adequate funding by (the various) state budgets, and an increase or no limit on giving from philanthropists and private donations. All of these things, of course, will eventually affect the status of black universities in the future, specifically their role in the black community and contribution to the enterprise of American mainstream higher education. Furthermore, and even more important, "If black colleges do not become content to surpass comparable white schools, they might demand a chance to show what they could deliver with equal resources. For, at this time, black students are still faced with an unhappy compromise between superior educational resources at white schools and the best chance for social participation at black institutions" (Fleming, 1984, p. 154). Ironically and in an important way, it is disappointing that there should be an occasion that:

> The black college is the only major American institution whose necessity is questioned by large numbers of people. It is the only American institution subjected to the suggestion that it self-destruct. . . . And yet the black college represents to black students what other schools traditionally associated with a particular religion outlook or ethnic group represent to other Americans – the availability of the choice of going to a school that embraces their past, their concerns, and their values (Jordan, 1975, p. 165).

And above all else, black colleges and universities will have to make the hard decisions necessary to ensure the future success of these institutions, such as not allowing the educational inequalities and economic disparities that exist with and between white colleges. Furthermore, one must take into account that few black institutions possess a solid financial base. But black schools must cover all of the bases. So the question that remains is: How would this be accomplished? By also insuring that the *productivity* of black colleges and universities is prodigious, and by taking all points of reference, and other aspects of their crowning scholarly achievements into view, the better off perhaps they will be. In other words, the most important achievement of black colleges and universities should be highlighted to appeal to the masses. Another important consideration is whether many of these black schools deserve the vituperative condemnation from critics that would have black institutions dismantled? Characteristically, as Jordan (1975, p. 165) astutely writes:

> Most crucial to the black community and the nation, is the continued survival of the black colleges. Their doors were open when white colleges would not allow blacks in, much less welcome them. Their doors are open today to masses of black students who cannot afford the high-cost of predominantly white institutions. The bulk of them are in the South, where the majority of black people still live. Generally, their students are poorer than those attending predominantly white colleges. Today, as in the past, the black colleges provide the training and dedication offered reluctantly, if at all, by their more prestigious brother institutions (Jordan 1975, p. 165).

Although black colleges and universities accommodate an expansive array of black needs, we must clearly understand that (many) black students that attend these institutions are not from the privileged classes, nor are they (or many) well prepared initially for college; therefore, what must be done to improve these educational discrepancies? Especially when "the college, like myriad other institutions, is established by the community to perform certain functions deemed essential to its survival" (Jones 1971, p. 734). On respective black campuses throughout the nation there is also a revolution of sorts going on. That is, black colleges and universities continue to clash with the fundamental assumptions about their *futility*. Indeed, their very indispensability is deeply troubling to many state higher educational school officials. Why should they continue in fact? A hard nose pragmatist would perhaps proclaim that there is no need to stop their existence. And one of the worst things our educational systems can do is to intersperse or fully integrate them with white institutions whose commitment to black students might not be necessarily a priority. In the final analysis, students and educators must recognize that:

> For thousand upon thousands of African Americans [black colleges] provided the only hope of acquiring higher education. Consequently, they have given the country most of its black intellectual leaders, as well as the great bulk of its black college graduates. What they accomplished is truly remarkable, and to allow them to whither away would be a major tragedy for African Americans and an impoverishment of American life (Waltman 1994, p. B1).

In the ultimate end, black colleges and universities provide poor blacks (or the educationally disadvantaged minority student) with a clear choice in the mainstream of American public higher education, as well as a supportive environment. According to Paulette V. Walker (1997, p. A 31), black colleges and universities also revive the struggling black or inner-city neighborhoods located around these venerable institutions. Finally, black students at predominantly black colleges and universities are not subjected to an increasingly hostile environment as at some white institutions (Haworth 1996, p. A 33). And in an atmosphere of learning, this will always be an important and crucial consideration. The black university, in the past, now, and in the future, reflects both our focus on black students and their advanced academic status in America's higher education system.

References

"Academic Curricular Developments in Black Colleges and Universities." 1978, May. A Study conducted by, *The National Association For Equal Opportunity in Higher Education*, supported by the Department of Health, Education, and Welfare, Region III.

Allen, Robert L. 1974, September. "Politics of the Attack On Black Studies." *The Black Scholar*. Vol. 6. No. 1.

Anderson, Ernest F. and Hrabowski, Freeman A. 1977, May/June. "Graduate School Success Of Black Students from White Colleges and Black Colleges." *The Journal of Higher Education*. Vol. XLVIII, No. 3.

Fleming, Jacqueline. 1984. *Blacks in College*. San Francisco: Jossey-Bass Publishers.

Gallagher, Buell G., Editor. 1971. *College And The Black Student: NAACP Tract For The Times*. New York: The Special Contribution Fund of the NAACP.

Green, Robert L. 1969, May. "The Black Quest for Higher Education: An Admissions Dilemma." *Personnel and Guidance Journal*. Vol. 47.

Haworth, Karla. 1996, October 4. "Continued Aid Sought For Black Colleges." *The Chronicle of Higher Education*.

Jones, Mack H. 1971. "The Responsibility of the Black College to the Black Community: Then and Now." *Daedalus*. Vol. 100.

Jordan, Vernon E. 1975. "Blacks and Higher Education – Some Reflections." *Daedalus*. Vol. 104.

Katz, Irwin and Greenbaum, Charles. 1963. "Effects of Anxiety, Threat, and Racial Environment On Task Performance of Negro College Students." *Journal of Abnormal and Social Psychology*. Vol. 66. No. 6.

LeMelle, Tilden J. and LeMelle, Wilbert J. 1969. *The Black College: A Strategy For Achieving Relevancy*. New York: Frederick A. Praeger.

Leo, John. 1998, March 8. "Blame For Low Test Score Rests Directly With Schools Methods." *Las Vegas Review-Journal*.

McGrath, Earl J. 1965. *The Predominantly Negro Colleges and Universities in Transition*. Teacher College, Columbia University: Bureau of Publications.

Parsons, Talcott and Platt, Gerald M. 1973. *The American University*. Cambridge, Massachusetts: Harvard University Press.

Reuben, Julie A. 1996. *The Making of The Modern University: Intellectual Transformation and the Marginalization of Morality*. Chicago: The University of Chicago Press.

Sowell, Thomas. 1993. *Inside American Education: The Decline, The Deception, The Dogmas*. New York: The Free Press.

Walker, Paulette V. 1997, June 13. "Black Colleges Help Revive Struggling
    Neighborhoods." *The Chronicle of Higher Education.*
Waltman, Jerold. 1994, July 6. "Assuring the Future of Black Colleges."
    The Chronicle of Higher Education.

Bibliography

Abarry, Shardow Abu. 1990, December 2. "Afrocentricity Introduction." *Journal of Black Studies*. Vol. 21.

"Academic Curricular Developments in Black Colleges and Universities." 1978, May. A study conducted by, *The National Association For Equal Opportunity in Higher Education*, supported by the Department of Health, Education, and Welfare, Region III.

Adams, Russell L.. 1980. "Evaluating Professionalism in the Context of Afro-American Studies." *The Western Journal of Black Studies*. Vol. 4, No. 2.

Adams, Russell L.. 1993, September 9. "Neophytes in Afrocentrism." *The Washington Post*.

Adler, Jerry, Manly, Howard, Smith, Nern E., Chideya, Farai, and Wilson, Larry. 1991, September. "African Dreams." *Newsweek*.

Allen, Robert L. 1974, September. "Politics of the Attack on Black Studies." *The Black Scholar*.

Anderson, Ernest F. and Hrabowski, Freeman A. 1977, May/June. "Graduate School Success of Black Students from White Colleges and Black Colleges." *The Journal of Higher Education*. Vol. XLVIII. No. 3.

Anderson, Tony. 1995. "Blowing Smoke: Exposing Empty Criticism of Afrocentricity." *Molefi Kete Asante and Afrocentricity: In Praise and Criticism*. Dhyana Ziegler, Editor. Nashville, Tennessee: James C. Winston Publishing Company.

Appiah, Anthony Kwame. 1993, February. "Europe Upside Down: Fallacies of the New Afrocentrism." *The Times Literary Supplement*.

Appiah, Anthony Kwame. 1997 October 9. "The Multiculturalist Misunderstanding." *The New York Review of Books*.

Applebee, Arthur N. 1996. *Curriculum As Conversation: Transforming Traditions of Teaching and Learning*. Chicago: The University of Chicago Press.

Applebome, Peter. 1997, June 18. "Rising College Costs Imperil the Nation, Blunt Report Says." *The New York Times*.

Asante, Molefi Kete. 1987. Black Flap of the book, *The Afrocentric Idea*. Pennsylvania: Temple University Press.

Asante, Molefi Kete. 1988. *Afrocentricity*. Trenton, New Jersey: Africa World Press, Inc.

Asante, Molefi Kete. 1990, November. "Battle Over Multicultural Education Rises In Intensity." *Education Week*.

Asante, Molefi Kete. 1990. *Kemet, Afrocentricity and Knowledge*. New Jersey: Africa World Press, Inc.

Asante, Molefi Kete. 1991, September. "Putting Africa at the Center." *Newsweek*.

Asante, Molefi Kete. 1992, Summer. "African American Studies: The Future of the Discipline." *The Black Scholar*. Vol. 16. No. 3.

Asante, Molefi Kete. 1996, July/August. "Ancient Truths: New Attacks of Afrocentrism Are As Weak As They Are False." *Emerge*.

Asante, Molefi Kete. 1996, March. "Reading Race in Antiquity: The Many Fallacies of Mary Lefkowitz." *Black Issues in Higher Education*.

Atwater, Deborah, F. 1995. "Asante and the Naming of Names: The Evolution of Rhetorical Concepts." In *Molefi Kete Asante and Afrocentricity: In Praise and Criticism*. Dhyana Ziegler, Editor. Nashville, Tennessee: Winston Derek Publishing Company.

Auster, Lawrence. 1991, May. "America Is in Danger of Losing its Soul." *Newsday*.

Baker, Houston, A., Jr. 1993. *Black Studies, Rap, and the Academy*. Chicago: The University of Chicago Press.

Bennett, Lerone, Jr. 1993. *Before the Mayflower: A History of Black America*. New York: Penguin Books.

Bernal, Martin, 1987. *Black Athena: The Afroasiatic Roots of Classical Civilization, Volume 1: The Fabrication of Ancient Greece 1785-1985*. New Jersey: Rutgers University Press.

Berry, Mary Frances and Blassingame, John. 1982. *Long Memory: The Black Experience in America*. New York: Oxford University Press.

"Black Colleges Step-up Recruitment." 1997, February 17. *Las Vegas Review-Journal*.

Bloom, Allan. 1987. *The Closing of the American Mind*. New York: Simon and Schuster, Inc.

Botstein, Leon. 1997. *Jefferson's Children: Education and the Promise American Culture*. New York: Doubleday.

Braddock II, Henry, Jomils and Dawkins, Marvin P. 1981. "Predicting Black Academics In Higher Education." *The Journal of Negro Education*. Vol. 50. No. 3.

Bran, Eva T. H. 1979. *Paradoxes of Education in a Republic*. Chicago: The University of Chicago Press.

Brown, Luther. 1992, October. "Recruits at HBCUs." *Black Enterprise*.

Browning, Smith, Jane E. and Williams, John B. 1978. "History and Goals of Black Institutions of Higher Learning." in *Black Colleges in America: Challenge, Development, Survival*. Charles V. Willie and Ronald E. Edmonds, editors. Teachers College, Columbia University, New York: Teachers College Press.

Brudney, Kent M., nd Culver, John H. 1998. *Critical Thinking and American Government*. Forth Worth, Texas: Harcourt Brace and Company.

Buchanan, Pat. 1997, July. "Losing America in the Multicultural Mix." *The Washington Times National Weekly Edition*.

Chamber, Julius L. 1993. "Brown v. Board of Education." *Race in America: The Struggle for Equality*, edited by Herbert Hill and James E. Jones, Jr. Madison, Wisconsin: The University of Wisconsin Press.

Colon, Alan K. 1984. "Critical Issues in Black Studies: A Selective Analysis." *Journal of Negro Education*. Vol. 53. No. 3.

Cooper, Kenneth J. 1992, November 27. "Broadening Horizons: Afrocentrism Takes Root in Atlantic Schools." *The Washington Post*.

Covin, David. 1990, December. "Afrocentricity In O Movimento Negro Unificado." *Journal of Black Studies*. Vol. 21.

Culotta, Elizabeth. 1992, November 13. "Black Colleges Cultivate Scientists." *Science*. Vol. 258.

Darling-Hammond, Linda. 1998, Spring. "Unequal Opportunity: Race and Education." *Brookings Review*. Vol. 16. No. 2.

Davies, Dick. 1994, March/April. "To Be Educated in the 1990s...Nevada Revamps its Core Curriculum." *Silver and Blue magazine*. Vol. 5. No. 4.

D' Souza, Dinesh. 1991. *Illiberal Education: The Politics of Race and Sex On Campus*. New York: The Free Press.

D'Souza, Dinesh. 1995. *The End of Racism: Principles For A Multicultural Society*. New York: The Free Press.

Early, Gerald. 1995. "Understanding Afrocentrism: Why Blacks Dream of a World Without Whites." *Civilization*.

Egan, Kieran. 1991. *The Educated Mind: How Cognitive Tools Shape Our Understanding*. Chicago: The University of Chicago Press.

Fields, Gary. 1995, September. "Controversy Begins With 'End' of Racism." *USA Today*.

Fleming, Jacqueline. 1984. *Blacks in College*. San Francisco, California: Jossey-Bass, Inc.

Franklin, John Hope, and Moss, Alfred, A. Jr. 1994. *From Slavery To Freedom: A History of African Americans*. New York: McGraw-Hill, Inc.

Freire, Paulo. 1972. *Pedagogy of the Oppressed*. New York: Herder and Herder.

Gallagher, Buell G., editor. 1971. *College and the Black Student: NAACP Tract For The Times*. New York: The Special Contribution Fund of the NAACP.

Garland, Sonja D. 1995. "Afrocentricity: Know the Truth of the Past for a Successful Future." In *Molefi Kete Asante and Afrocentricity: In Praise and Criticism*. Dhyana Ziegler, Editor. Nashville, Tennessee: James C. Winston Derek.

Gates, Henry Louis. 1991, September. "Beware of the New Pharaohs." *Newsweek*.

Gill, Walter. 1991. *Issues in African American Education*. Nashville, Tennessee: Winston-Derek Publishers, Inc.

Glazer, Nathan. 1997. *We Are All Multiculturalist Now*. Massachusetts: Harvard University Press.

Green, Dan S. and Driver, Edwin D., editors. 1978. *W.E.B. DuBois: On Sociology and the Black Community*. Chicago: The University of Chicago Press.

Green, Robert L. 1969, May. "The Black Quest for Higher Education: An Admissions Dilemma." *Personnel and Guidance Journal*. Vol. 47.

Gwynne, S.C. 1997, June. "Back to the Future." *Time Magazine*.

Harlan, Zouis R. 1983. *Booker T. Washington: The Wizard of Tuskegee 1901-1915*. New York: Oxford University Press.

Haworth, Karla. 1996, October 4. "Continued Aid Sought For Black Colleges." *The Chronicle of Higher Education*.

Herskovits, Melville J. 1948, January-March. "The Contribution of Afro-American Studies to Africanist Research." *American Anthropologist*. Vol. 50. No. 1.

Hill, Kathleen T. and Hill, Gerald N. 1994. *Real Life Dictionary of American Politics*. Los Angeles: General Publishing Group.

Hilliard, Asa G. 1988. "Conceptual Confusion and the Persistence of Group Oppression Through Education." *Equality and Excellence: The University of Massachusetts School of Education Quarterly*. Vol. 24. No. 1.

Holloway, Joseph E. 1990. *Africanism in American Culture*. Bloomington and Indianapolis: Indiana University Press.

Hooks, Bell. 1994. *Teaching to Transgress: Education as the Practice of Freedom*. New York: Routledge.

Hooks, Bell and West, Cornel. 1993, September 4. "Afrocentric Program Gets Go-Ahead." *The Washington Post*.

Hooks, Bell and West, Cornel. 1991. Breaking Bread: *Insurgent Black Intellectual Life*. Boston, Massachusetts: South End Press.

Hughes, Langston, Meltzer, Milton, Lincoln, Eric C., Spencer, Michael Jon. 1995. *A Pictorial History of African Americans*. 6th Edition. New York: Crown Publishers, Inc.

Jackson, Kennell. 1996. *America Is Me: 170 Fresh Questions and Answers On Black American History*. New York: Harper Collins.

Jalata, Asafa. 1995. "African American Nationalism, Development, and Afrocentricity: Implications for the Twenty-First Century." In *Molefi Kete Asante and Afrocentricity: In Praise and in Criticism*. Dhyana Ziegler, Editor. Nashville, Tennessee: James Winston Publishing Company, Inc.

Janice, Elizabeth. 1992, August. "1st in Black Degrees." *Black Enterprise*.

Jones, Mack H. 1971. "The Responsibility of the Black College to the Black Community: Then and Now." *Daedalus*. Vol 100.

Jones, Terry. 1998, July-August. "Life After Proposition 209: Affirmative Action May Be Dying, But the Dream Lives On." *Academe*. Vol. 84. No. 4.

Jordan, Vernon E. 1975. "Blacks and Higher Education - Some Reflections." *Daedalus*. Vol. 104.

Kannerstein, Gregory. 1978. "Black Colleges: Self-Concept," in *Black Colleges in America: Challenge, Development Survival*. Charles V. Willie and Ronald R. Edmonds, editors. Teachers College, Columbia University, New York: Teachers College Press.

Karenga, Maulana. 1993. *Introduction to Black Studies*. Los Angeles, California: The University of Sankore Press.

Katz, Irwin and Greenbaum, Charles. 1963. "Effects of Anxiety, Threat, and Racial Environment On Task Performance of Negro College Students." *Journal of Abnormal and Social Psychology*. Vol. 66. No. 6.

Kershaw, Terry. 1992, Winter. "Afrocentrism and the Afrocentric Method." *The Western Journal of Black Studies*. Vol. 16. No. 3.

Kershaw, Terry. 1989. "The Emerging Paradigm in Black Studies." *The Western Journal of Black Studies*. Vol. 13. No. 1.

Lefkowitz, Mary. 1992, February. "Not Out of Africa: The Origins of Greece of Africa: The Origins of Greece and the Illusions of Afrocentrists." *The New Republic*.

Lefkowitz, Mary. 1996. *Not Out of Africa: How Afrocentrism Became And Excuse To Teach Myth As History*. New York: Basic Books.

Leman, N. 1993, January. "Black Nationalism on Campus." *The Atlantic Monthly*.

LeMelle, Tilden J. and LeMelle, Wilbert J. 1969. *The Black College: A Strategy For Achieving Relevancy*. New York: Frederick A. Praeger.

Leo, John. 1998. "Blame For Low Test Scores Rests Directly With School Methods." *Las Vegas Review-Journal*.

Lewis, Anthony. 1998, May 18. "Turn of the Tide." *The New York Times*.

Levine, Lawrence W. 1996. *The Opening of the American Mind: Canons, Culture, and History*. Boston, Massachusetts: Beacon Press.

Lindsey, Howard O. 1994. *A History Of Black America*. Secaucus, New Jersey: Chartwell Books, Inc.

Litwack, Leon F. 1996. "The Making of A Historian," in *Historians and Race: Autobiography and the Writing of History*. Indianapolis: Indiana University Press.

Magner, Denise K. 1997, April 18. "Deep Rifts Divide Faculty in Temple University's Afrocentric Ph. D. Program." *The Chronicle of Higher Education*.

Manne, Henry G. 1978. "The Political Economy of Modern Universities," in *Education In a Free Society*. Anne Husted Burleigh, Editor. 2nd Printing. Indianapolis, Indiana: Liberty Press.

Martin, Guy and Young, Carlene. 1984. "The Paradox of Separate and Unequal: African Studies and Afro-American Studies." *Journal of Negro Education*. Vol. 53. No. 3.

Mays, Benjamin E. 1978. "The Black College in Higher Education," in *Black Colleges in Colleges in America: Challenge, Development, Survival*. Charles V. Willie and Ronald R. Edmonds, editors. Teachers College, Columbia University, New York: Teachers College Press.

McGrath, Earl J. 1965. *The Predominantly Negro Colleges and Universities in Transition*. Teachers College, Columbia University: Bureau of Publications.

Mercer, Joye. 1996, April 12. "A Struggling Campus Turns to Prayer." *The Chronicle of Higher Education*.

Mills, Denise K. 1997, April 18. "Deep Rifts Divide Faculty in Temple University's Afrocentric Ph.D. Program." *The Chronicle of Higher Education*.

Monges, Miriam Ma'at-Ka-Re. 1997, June 6. "Africology at Temple University." *The Chronicle of Higher Education*.

Neustadt, R. E., and May, Ernest R. 1986. *Thinking In Time: The Uses of History for Decision Makers*. New York: The Free Press.

Newby, I. A. 1969, January. "Historians and Negroes." *The Journal of Negro History*.

Nicklin, Julie L. 1993, March 10. "Financial Troubles at Small Black Colleges Raise Questions About Role of Their Trustees in Overseeing Management." *The Chronicle of Higher Education*.

O'Reilly, Kenneth. 1994. *Black Americans: The FBI File*. David Gallen, Editor. New York: Carroll and Graf Publishers, Inc.

Parsons, Talcott and Platt, Gerald M. 1973. *The American University*. Cambridge, Massachusetts: Harvard University Press.

Postman, Neir. 1996. *The End of Education: Redefining the Value of School*. New York: Alfred A. Knopf.

Poe, Richard. 1997. *Black Spark, White Fire: Did African Explorers Civilize Ancient Europe?* Rocklin, California: Prima Publishing.

Quarles, Benjamin. 1971. *The Negro in the Making of America*. New York: The Macmillan Company.

Rampersad, Arnold. 1990. *The Art and Imagination of W.E.B. DuBois*. New York: Schocken Books.

Reuben, Julie A. 1996. *The Making of the Modern University: Intellectual Transformation and the Marginalization of Morality*. Chicago: The University of Chicago Press.

Roebuck, J. B., and Murty, K. S. 1993. *Historically Black Colleges and Universities: Their Place in American Higher Education*. Westport, Connecticut: Praeger.

Rogers, MacLean. 1994, August/September. "Racism, and Antisemitism in the Classroom." *Midstream*. Vol. 40. No. 6.

Sailer, Steve. 1997, March 10. "Black-to-Back Blacks." *National Review*.

Shea, Christopher. 1997 May 9. "For These Scholarly Authors, More Is Better: A Few Prolific Professors Take Great Pride in Writing Book After Book." *The Chronicle of Higher Education.*

Shea, Christopher. 1997, April 11. "Multiculturalism Gains An Unlikely Supporter." *The Chronicle of Higher Education.*

Sheppard, Nathaniel, Jr. 1994, July 24. "Black College Enrollments Soar on Pride." *Pacific Stars and Stripes.*

Sidel, Ruth. 1994. *Battling Bias: The Struggle for Identity and Community on College Campuses.* New York: Penguin Books.

Sleeper, Jim. 1997. *Liberal Racism.* New York: Viking Penguin.

Sowell, Thomas. 1993. *Inside American Education: The Decline, The Deception, The Dogmas.* New York: The Free Press.

Specter, Michael. 1990, February 26. "Was Nefertiti Black? Bitter Debate Erupts." *The Washington Post.*

Steele, Claude M. 1992, April. "Race and the Schooling of Black Americans." *The Atlantic Monthly.*

Stein, Herbert. 1998, February 24. "A Model of Philanthropy." *The Wall Street Journal.*

Steward, Jeffrey C. 1996. *1001 Things Everyone Should Know About African American History.* New York: Doubleday.

"Study Shows More Minority Students Enrolling in College." 1996, June 10. *Las Vegas Review-Journal.*

Stringer, Christopher and Mckie, Robin. 1996. *African Exodus: The Origins of Modern Humanity.* New York: Henry Holt and Company.

Takaki, Ronald. 1993. *A Different Mirror: History of Multicultural America.* New York: Little, Brown and Company.

The Original African Heritage Study Bible. 1993. Nashville, Tennessee: The James C. Winston Publishing Company.

Tonsor, Stephen J. 1978. "Authority, Power, and the University," in *Education in a Free Society.*

Uriate, Mercedes Lynn de. 1997, September 16. "Lack of Color Becoming A Pattern On University Scene." *Las Vegas Review-Journal.*

Veysey, Laurence R. 1965. *The Emergence of the American University.* Chicago: The University of Chicago Press.

Wagener, Ursula and Smith, Edgar E. 1993, January/February. "Maintaining A Competitive Edge: Strategic Planning for Historically Black Institutions." *Change.*

Walker, Paulette V. 1997, June 13. "Black Colleges Help Revive Struggling Neighborhoods. *The Chronicle of Higher Education.*

Waltman, Jerold. 1994, July 6. "Assuring the Future of Black Colleges." *The Chronicle of Higher Education.*

Washington, Booker T. 1995 edition. *Up From Slavery.* New York: Oxford University Press.

Warren, Kenneth W. 1993. *Black and White Strangers: Race and American Literary Realism.* Chicago: The University of Chicago Press.

Wenglinsky, Harold. 1997. *Students at Historically Black Colleges and Universities: Their Aspirations and Accomplishments.* Princeton, New Jersey: Policy Information Center at the Education Testing Service (ETS).

Wexler, Sanford. 1993. *The Civil Rights Movement: An Eyewitness History.* New York: Facts On File, Inc.

Whitaker, Charles. 1992, March. "Black Colleges At the Crossroads." *Ebony.*

Wickham, DeWayne. 1993, June. "Stop Blaming the Victims for Black Separatism." *USA Today.*

Will, George F. 1996, February 19. "Intellectual Segregation." *Newsweek.*

Wilson, Reginald. 1992, Spring. Book review of *Fostering Minority Access and Achievement in Higher Education.* San Francisco: Jossey-Bass, 1987, by Richard C. Richardson, in *Harvard Educational Review.* Vol. 62. No. 1.

Wilson, William Julius. 1996. *When Work Disappears: The World of the New Urban Poor.* New York: Alfred A. Knopf.

Woodson, Carter G. 1933 and 1969. *Mis-education of the Negro.* Washington, D.C.: The Associate Publishers, Inc.

Index

Abarry, Abu Shardow, 78, 79
academically rigorous, 98
Academic concerns, 115
    (performance, excellence)
academic opportunities, 31
accommodationist, 15, 19
Adams, Russell, 54, 83
Adler, Jerry, 66
administrators, 103
admissions, 113
aesthetics, 25, 49, 67, 71, 83
    (aesthetic vision)
Affirmative Action, 3, 33, 48, 100,
    101, 103, 113
African American and African
    History, 24, 66, 67, 68, 69, 70,
    71, 78, 81
African American colleges and
    universities, 34
African Americans, and students, 1,
    2, 3, 9, 10, 16, 20, 21, 23, 32,
    41, 42, 56, 68, 78, 84, 91, 93,
    94, 95, 96, 97, 101, 102, 103,
    109, 110, 111, 122 ,
African American (scholarly)
    community, 74, 83
African ancestry, 82, 85
African and Afrocentric thought, 73,
    76
African (black) semantics, 64
African-centered knowledge, 80
African-centered perspective, and
    culture, 56, 65, 66, 68, 76
African heritage, 83, 84
African historical experience, 85
African history and knowledge, 76
African intelligentsia, 11
Africanists, 70
African phenomenon, 84
African theory, 84
Africology, 3, 84, 85
Afro-American Council, 18

Afroamerican societies, 54
Afro- and African-American
    Studies, 12, 33, 53, 54, 56, 66,
    80, 82
Afroasiatic, 79
Afro-centric complex, and
    enterprise, 71, 85
Afrocentric ideas, concept, 71, 73
Afrocentricity, 3, 34, 56, 63, 64,
    65, 66, 67, 68, 69, 70, 71, 72,
    73, 75, 76, 77, 80, 81, 82, 83,
    84, Afrocentric, 85
Afrocentric myth, 75
Afrocentrism, 64, 65, 66, 67, 68,
    70, 71, 73, 74, 75, 76, 77, 78,
    79, 80, 81, 82, 83, 84, 85
Afrocentrists, 65, 73, 74, 75, 76,
    77, 78, 79, 80, 81, 82, 83, 84
agricultural and technical training,
    37
Alabama, Tuskegee, 21
Alcorn Agricultural and Mechanical
    Colleges, 31
Allen, Robert, 58
America education complex, 71
American citizenship, 93
American culture, 47
American democracy, 101
Amcrican educators, 99
American Enterprise Institute, 24,
    73
American history, 104
American identity, 72
American institutions, 120, 121
American intellectual life, 9
American philosophy, 102
American Universities, 96
Andrews, William, 10, 13
antifeminist, 55
Anti-Semitic, 72
Appiah, Kwame Anthony, 71
Applebee, 3

136 *Index*

approach to admissions, 103
Asante, Kariamu Welsh, 63
Asante, Molefi Kete, 56, 63, 64, 65,
    66, 67, 68, 69, 70, 72, 73, 75,
    76, 82, 83, 84, 85
Asian Americans, 84
Atlanta compromise speech, 21
Atlanta University, 25, 110
at-risks black students, 96, 119
Atwater, Deborah, 64
Auster, Lawrence, 72
axiological, 67
Ayers v. Mabus, 99, 100
baccalaureate institutions, 97
bachelors degrees, 42
Baker, Houston, 55
Baptists, 92
Bennett, Lerone, 17, 35
Bernal, Martin, 74, 79, 80
Berry, Mary Frances, 15, 36, 37,
    38, 40
Bill of Rights, 21
biracial education, 113
black aesthetic, 11
black alumni, 36
black American culture, 94
black Americans, 93, 119, 120
Black American scholarship, 56
black churches, 35, 39
black, college-educated middle
    classes, 34, 35
black colleges and universities, 34,
    35, 37, 38, 40, 41, 42, 50, 91,
    92, 93, 95, 96, 97, 98, 99, 100,
    101, 102, 103, 104, 105, 109,
    111, 114, 115, 116, 117, 118,
    120, 121, 122, 123
Black communication, 66
black communities, 36, 39, 101,
    113, 114, 117, 118, 122
black conservatives, 23
black culture, 68
black education, 34

black enrollments, 112
black experience, 11, 50, 51, 59,
black feminism, 52, 53, 55, 56, 58,
    59
black heritage, and history, 43, 49,
    50
black history, 117
black institutions of higher learning,
    30, 33, 34, 35, 36, 37, 40, 41,
    42, 43, 91, 92, 93, 94, 95, 96,
    97, 98, 99, 100, 101, 102, 103,
    104, 109, 112, 115, 116, 118,
    119
black intellectuals, 10, 11, 14, 22,
    25, 34, 52
black interest in education, 109
black leadership, 43, 103
black-liberal education, 11
black liberals, 23
black life experiences, 85
black lodges, 35
black males, 98
black nationalism, black nation, 13,
    14
black people, 85
black scholar(s), 16, 18, 82
black schools, 114, 117, 118, 119,
    121
black students, 5, 10, 30, 31, 37,
    41, 53, 58, 95, 96, 97, 98, 99,
    103, 104, 109, 113, 114, 115,
    116, 121, 122, 123
Black Studies programs,
    departments, and Black Studies
    movement, 47, 48, 49, 50, 51,
    52, 53, 54, 55, 56, 58, 59, 72
black university, 119, 123
Blassingame, John, 15, 36, 37, 38,
    40
Bloom, Allan, 2, 4
boards of higher education, 96
Botstein, Leon, 94
Brudney, Kent, 49, 58

Buchanan, Pat, 69
buildings and facilities, 99
business-oriented, 100
California, 48
California State University, 56
campuses, American, 2
Canada, Niagara Falls, 22
canon of scholarship, 53
Carnegie, Andrew, 18
charlatans, 70
church-related colleges, or church-
    supported institutions, 37, 39
circumstantial evidence, 79
City College in New York, 52
civilizations, African, 70
civil rights, movement, 14, 22, 91
civil rights activists, 13, 113
civil war, 10, 13, 39, 68, 92
Cleopatra, 74
college, 36, 113
college education, 37
college enrollment, 115
college graduates, 100
college students, 113
Colon, Alan, 50, 59, 70
colonizer, colonized, 53
color-blind society, 72
communications revolution, 32, 71
Communist Party, 25
community politics, 114
Confederate States, 39
conformist tendencies, 114
Congress, 103
conservative academicians, 71
conservative black scholars, 67
conservatives, 52, 56
constitution, U.S., 21
contemporary life, 101
CORE, 22
Cornell University, 74, 79
cosmological, 67
Covin, David, 71
Crisis magazine, 12, 25

Culotta, Elizabeth, 91
cultural context, 81
cultural deprivation, 111
cultural identity, 80
Culver, John, 49, 58
curriculums, curricula, 2, 5, 34, 43,
    49, 50, 51, 52, 57, 58, 65, 66,
    68, 93, 113, 114, 115
Darling-Hammond, Linda, 93
deep south, 38
degree of alienation, 113
democratization, 31
desegregation, 14
detractors, 80, 112
diaspora, 24, 48, 56, 64, 68, 82, 85
dilettantes, 56, 82
discrimination, 110, 113
disenfranchisement, 18
dissenters, 71, 80, 83
District of Columbia, 22
diversity, 3, 57
dominant power structure, and
    culture, 36, 37, 56
dominate white culture, 111, 113
    regime
Driver, Edwin, 12, 13, 22
D'Souza, Dinesh, 33, 50, 51, 52,
    73, 74
Dubois, William Edward B., 1, 9,
    10, 11, 12, 13, 14, 15, 16, 17,
    18, 19, 20, 21, 22, 23, 24, 25,
    35
Early, Gerald, 72, 83, 85
economic independence, 10
education, 4, 85
educational discrepancies, 122
educational environments, 54
educational experiences, 91, 99
educational goals, 118
educational ideas, 3, 4
educational inconsistencies, 93
    resources
educational institutions in America,
    118

educational issues, American, 35
educational opportunity, 97, 111, 116
educational organizations, 100
educational philosophy, 10, 40
educational politics, 98
educational programs, 98
educational school systems, 100, 122 and officials
educational systems, 5, 30, 42, 93,
Education, higher, 3, 4, 5, 12, 31, 33
education-related charities, 100
educators, 100, 102, 111, 122
egalitarianism, 103
Egypt, 71, 72, 73, 74, 75, 76, 79, 82 (Egyptian)
elitist standards, 99
epistemology, epistemological, 67, 70
equality of opportunity, 91, 94
equal rights, 14
equal status, 110
esoteric educational things, 49
ethnic chauvinism, 72, 78 ethnic determinism
ethnic groups, 2, 5, 58, 121
ethnic studies, 3, 5, 54
ethnocentrism, 72
etymologies, 80
eurocentric, 5, 50, 51, 52, 65, 68, 69, 78
Eurocentric education, 52
eurocentric notion, 83
Eurocentric perspective, 67, 69, 82
Eurocentrism, 71
European core, 69
European dominance, 72, 76 culture, and European-centered teaching methods
Europeans, 69, 76, 77
European thought, 71
European truimphalism, 76

European worldview, and point of view, 79, 82
Evers, Medgar, 36
FBI, 25
federal aid, 103
federal employment, 100
federal government, 119
federal grants, 110
federal recruiting, 100
Feminist, 48, 51, 55, 56 (Feminism)
financial aid and support, 93, 98 woes
Fisk University, 9, 38, 110
fist-rate schools, 110
Florida Agriculture and Mechnical, 37
foreign civilizations, 82
Franklin, John Hope, 16, 39, 41, 42
Freedman's Bureau, 35, 38, 39
Freire, Paulo, 2, 4, 52, 54
Gates, Henry Louis, 12, 64, 73, 74, 80, 82
George Mason University, 18
Ghana, 25
Ghanian intellectual, 71
Gill, Walter, 32, 34
Glazer, Nathan, 72, 101
global markets, 32
graduates, 115, 122
grandfather clause, 18
Greece, 73, 79
Greek civilization, 75
Greek classicist, 75
Greek, scholars, 73
Greeks, 74, 75, 76, 79, 82
Green, Dan, 12, 13, 22
Gwynne, S.C., 48
Hampton Institute, 10, 39
Harlan, Louis, 19, 20
Harvard University, 9, 12, 25, 40, 64, 71
HBCU campuses, 100

hegemony, 78
Heidegger, 83
Herodotus, 79
Herskovits, Melville, 54
heterogenous atmosphere, 99
higher academic standard, 117
higher education, 94, 95, 103, 104, 105, 109, 110, 111, 113, 114, 117, 118
higher educational degrees, 119
higher educational institutions, 70, 92, 93
higher educational (school) system, 37, 40, 47, 49, 56, 59, 100, 109, 111, 112, 116 (and academia)
higher education for negroes, 115
higher learning, 59, 94, 113
Hilliard, Asa, 58, 83
Hispanics, 48, 51, 84
historically black colleges and universities (HBCUs), 29, 30, 31, 32, 33, 35, 36, 40, 42, 91, 95, 97, (And institutions) 100, 109, 116
historical methodology, 77, 78
historiographical proof, 79
history, American, 71
history, black, 72
holistic approach, 50
hooks, bell, 52, 53, 55
Howard University, 38, 39, 102, 110
humanistic training, 32, 55 (humanist)
humanizing function, 67
human orientation, 71
ideologies of blackness, 73
impoverished political subjects, 110
impoverishment of American life, 122
incendiary crackpots, 70
industrial art, 115

industrial training, 10, 17, 20
inner-city neighborhoods, 123
institutional racist situations, 59
institutions of higher learning, 98
integrated schools, 84
integration, 10, 43
intellectual tools, 112
inter-cultural understanding, 79
inter-group relations, 119
interpersonal relationships, 71
irrefutable scholarly research, 79
Italians, 84
Jackson, Kennell, 24
Jackson State University, 102
Jalata, Asafa, 22
Janice, Elizabeth, 95
Jewish philanthropists, 40
Jews, 84
Jim Crow, 22
Jones, Mack, 110, 114
Jones, Terry, 3, 5
Jordan, Vernon, 113, 122
Kannerstein, Gregory, 98
Karenga, Maulana, 56, 83
Kemetic (Egyptian) civilization, 66
Kershaw, Terry, 59, 67
King, Martin Luther, 36
knowledge-in-action, 3, 4
knowledge-out-of-context, 3
Ku Klux Klan, 19
Kush, 73
Kwanzaa, 56
land-grant institutions, 38
leaders, community, 114
leadership, 13
leadership, African American, 14
Lefkowitz, Mary, 75, 76, 77, 79, 80
legends, 81
legitimacy, legitimate, legitimize, 83, 101, 113, 118
LeMelle, Tilden, 119
LeMelle, Wilbert, 119
Leo, John, 120, 121

Levine, Lawrence, 47, 57
Lewis, Anthony, 103
Liberal arts education, 1
liberal bias, 52
liberal detractors, 82
liberal scholars, 119
liberating praxis, 55
Lindsey, Howard, 38, 39
Litwack, Leon, 11
Locke, John, 51
Luisiana legislature, 18
Madison, 51
mainstream American culture, 84,
    121, 123
Manne, Henry, 31
Marshall, Thurgood, 36
Martin, Guy, 53, 58
Marxist pragmatics, 75
May, Ernest, 1
Mayflower, 69
Mays, Benjamin, 101
McGrath, Earl, 104, 116
Mediterranean world, 79
meliorism, 22
Mercer, Joye, 92, 93
method, Afrocentric, 65, 67, 75
    (Eurocentric)
method of analysis, 84
middle class values, 112
minority groups, 2
minority leaders, and students, 51,
    97, 103
minority student enrollment, 96
minority students, 123
missionary groups, 35
missionary zeal, 40
mode, Eurocentric, 68
Morehouse University, 110
Morrill Act, 37, 38
Morrison, Toni, 36
Moss, Alfred, 16, 41, 42
multicultural, 4, 5
multicultural education, 72

Multiculturalism, 50, 51, 56, 72
Mydral, Gunnar, 74
NAACP, 9, 12, 22, 23, 25
National Association For Equal
    Opportunity in Higher
    Education (NAFEO), 115
Negro (black) youth, 111
Negro colleges and universities, 98,
    112, 119
Negroes, college-trained, 15, 16
Negroes liberal arts colleges, 16,
    119
Negro scholar, 34
Negro scholarship, 34
neo-separatism, 117
Neustadt, Richard, 1
Newby, I.A., 49
new racism, 49
New World Negro, 54
Niagara Movement, 22
Nile Valley, 66
non-white, 81
Norman, Jessye, 36
North Carolina Agricultural and
    Technical State University, 102
Nubia, 73
Oberlin University, 40
Office of Personnel Management,
    100 (OPM)
opportunity gap, 111
paradigms, 76
parity, 95
Parks, Rosa, 36
Parsons, Talcott, 33
pedagogical tools, 81
pedagogy, 11, 55
Pennsylvania, 112
Ph.D. program in black studies, 83
philanthropist, philanthropic
    organizations, 18, 19, 31, 38,
    40, 41, 100, 109, 121
philosophic mode, 70 (philosophy)
philosophic understanding, 4, 71

Plato, 51, 74
Platt, Gerald, 33
pluralistic nation, 81
pluralistic society, 32
pluralists, 72
polarizing and political fraught arenas, 95
political action, 22
political and educational battles, 111
political rights, 110
political spotlight, 103
politicians, 94, 100
politicizing education, 94
popular music (Rap and Rock), 30
Postman, Neil, 30, 104
poverty, 111
pragmatic, 22
pragmatist, 122
predominantly black institute, 113
preferences, 5, 109, 113
preferential treatment, 33
prejudicial scholarship, 54
premier public universities, 103
private black colleges, 41, 117
private donations, 121
privilege classes, 122
problem-solving and problem-posing education, 54, 55
progressive experiments, 103
prophetic insight, 5
Proposition, 209, 95
pseudo-scholar, and pseudo-scholarly work, scholarship, 73, 78, 80
pseudo-teaching, 71
pseudo-thinking, 71
public-controlled college for Negroes, 41
public intellectual, 16
Pullman cars, 18
Quarles, Benjamin, 15, 16, 22, 37, 38
quasi-scholarly approach, 74

race-blind, 103, 113
race card, 59
race-conscious, society, 115
race-relations, 11, 14, 74, 119
racial antagonism, 14
racial dynamite, 73
racial groups, or racial minorities, 2, 6, 49, 54, 58
racialism, 23
racial isolationist, 36
racial preference programs, 31, 109
racial vagaries of life, 96
racism, 10, 11, 75, 96, 110
racist attitudes, 92
radical blacks, 1
Rampersad, Arnold, 20
Rashad, Phylicia, 36
Ravitch, Diane, 72
Reconstruction, 12, 39, 40
religion, 71
religious orientation, 71
remedial training, 118
Republic, 110
residual conformist, 114
Reuben, Julie, 109
right-wing, 73
Rosenwald, Julius, 19, 40
Sartre, 83
Schlesinger, Arthur, 78, 81
Scholarship, African, 79, 82, 117
school reform, 109
school tradition, 2
science, 71
scientific racism, 54
Sears, Roebuck and Company, 40
second-class citizens, 37
segregation, 2, 14, 18, 113
self-awareness, 3
Selma University in Alabama, 92, 93
separatism, 113
Shea, Christopher, 84
Sidel, Ruth, 57

slaves, 37, 38
Sleeper, Jim, 73
Smith, Edgar, 97, 102
social agendas, 103
socialization agents, 113
social participation, 121
Southern plantations, 39
southern states, 112
Southern University Agricultural
    and Mechanical College, 102
Southern White Democrats, 38
Sowell, Thomas, 34, 49, 50, 51,
    101, 112
state and local governemt, 35
state supported historically black
    institutions, 99
Steele, Claude, 98
Stein, Herbert, 24
Stewart, Jeffrey, 18
strategic planning, 102
students, African American, 2, 3, 4,
    5, 29, 43
sub-human, 111
Sub-Saharan Africa, 73
Sullivan, Louis, 36
Talented Tenth, 22
teachers, 4
teaching academic skills, 101
teaching holistically, 52
technological advancements, 114
Temple University in Philadelhia,
    66, 67, 74
Tennessee Agricultural and
    Industrial, 37
Texas, 48, 112
Third World studies, 33, 56
    (models)
traditional European-centered
    teaching, 71
traditionalist-conservative, 15
traditional method, 67
traditional research universities, 110
trustees, 100

Tuskegee Institute, 10, 12, 15, 18,
    19, 24, 40
uneducable, 111, 114
United Negro College Fund, 93
United States, 40, 43, 53, 55, 58,
    74, 94, 95, 101, 109, 110, 116,
    117, 119
universities, 5, 50, 109, 111, 113,
    114 (and university)
university activities, 2
University of Berlin, 9
University of California, 95
University of Maryland, 19
University of Pennsylvania, 55
University of Southern Mississippi,
    110
university systems, 2
unorthodox ideas, 80
vituperative condemnation, 121
vocational education, and training,
    1, 10, 17, 22
Wagner, Ursula, 97, 102
Walker, Alice, 36
Walker, Paulette, 123
Waltman, Jerold, 110
Warren, Kenneth, 20
Washington, Booker T., 1, 9, 10,
    11, 12, 13, 14, 15, 16, 17, 18,
    19, 20, 21, 22, 23, 24, 25, 40
Wellesley College, 75
Wenglinsk, Harold, 35
Western civilization, 47, 68, 71, 72,
    76, 79, 82, 112
Western culture, 72, 75
Western ethos, 70
Western music, 30
Whitaker, Charles, 92
White American campuses, 33
White Americans, 15, 40, 51
White colleges and universities, 29,
    30, 35, 41, 42, 43, 48, 50, 97,
    110, 113, 114, 117, 122
white flight, 84

white institutions, 34, 92, 109, 113,
    114, 123
White Racism, 78
white scholars, 68, 82
Wickham, DeWayne, 30
Wilder, Douglas, 36
Will, George, 77, 78
Wilson, William Julius, 17
Winfrey, Oprah, 36
Woodson, Carter, 4, 5
Yale, 40
Young, Andrew, 36
Young, Carlene, 53, 58

About the Author

EARNEST N. BRACEY is a retired Army Lieutenant Colonel, with over twenty years of active military service. He was commissioned through Reserve Officer Training (**Distinguished Military Graduate**) at Jackson State University, where he graduated with honors (**Magna Cum Laude**), and received his bachelor of arts degree in political science, in 1974. He also received the master of arts degree in Public Administration, in 1979, from Golden Gate University, a master of arts degree in International Affairs, in 1983, from the Catholic University of America, and his doctorate of Public Administration (with emphasis in Public Policy), in 1993, from George Mason University.

A recipient of numerous military awards and honors, he is also a graduate of the United States Naval War College and the Command and General Staff College at Fort Leavenworth, Kansas, and previously served as Director of Administration at the prestigious Industrial College of the Armed Forces, Washington, D. C.

Dr. Bracey serves as Nevada's chairperson for the National Association of African-American Studies, and currently teaches political science and Black American History at the Community College of Southern Nevada in Las Vegas. His work has appeared in professional Journals and other publications, and he co-authored the book, *American Politics and Culture Wars* (1997). He is also the author of the novels, *Choson* (1994), and *The Black Samurai (1998).*